Love, Charles

Tricia Cundiff

Love, Charles

Copyright © 2022 by Tricia Cundiff. All Rights Reserved.

All rights reserved. No part of this book may be reproduced in any form or by any electronic or mechanical means including information storage and retrieval systems, without permission in writing from the author. The only exception is by a reviewer, who may quote short excerpts in a review.

ISBN 978-1-7340359-9-5

This book is based upon the actual letters written by Charles Poag during his service during World War II. Neither the author nor contributors shall be held liable or responsible for any loss or damage allegedly arising from any suggestion or information contained in this book.

Tricia Cundiff
Visit my website at www.TriciaCundiff.com

Printed in the United States of America

First Printing: November 2022

From the Author:

Love, Charles began with a dear woman asking me to read the letters her father had written to his mother (her grandmother) during the years of World War II, and perhaps compile them into a story. And so began a journey through the eyes of a young man, away from home and familiarity and thrust into the arms of government desperate to conquer the evil that invaded lands across the oceans, and our own Pearl Harbor. The letters grew into a moving tale of new experiences, anticipation and regret, fear and hope.

This story is based on actual events, as the pages include excerpts of the letters written, experiences and events passed down by word of mouth to relatives and the daughters of Charles and Louise, Jennie and Priscilla, and sources from historical references. Many actual names have been replaced, primarily because they are now unknown. Apologies to those that should be represented here as acquaintances and confidants of Charles and Louise.

The historical segments from World War II serve to give you, the reader, the context of the time. As days gone by, and wars forever fought now on a different playing field, this will hopefully give some clarity to the era.

Many thanks to Chad Lloyd, whose editing and publishing make this possible, Gayle Haliburton, a gentle and kind reminder of correct phrasing and so much encouragement, and to Jennie and Priscilla, for allowing me to be part of this journey.

As is only appropriate, Jennie and Priscilla, will make the dedication. For my part, I applaud the families across our great land that have given much, and continue to give of themselves in the name of God, family, and country. God bless you.

Respectfully,
Tricia Cundiff

The heartfelt dedication of this beautifully written chronicle of the lives, loves and faith of our father and mother, Charles and Louise Poag, is given with honor and appreciation to all members, past and present, of the Poag and Ramsay families. Charles and Louise represented many couples of the 1940s, concerned for their country and their family, and above all, committed to giving their best.

To those who told us stories and taught us about the era in which they lived, and to our parents for their love and Christian example, we are forever grateful.

-Jennie & Priscilla

PROLOGUE

The tall man gazed at the scene before him but saw something different. The view had changed somewhat since his first arrival here as a young man, a much younger man. Still a boy, really.

The voices brought him to the present; he shook his head as if to sweep away the cobwebs of memory. The woman he loved with all his heart walked ahead, laughing. Their daughters walked beside her. They looked like their mother; even their voice was hers. The gate was close by; he pulled his ID from his pocket. They would need it to get in. The military base had changed quite a bit. He hoped his girls would never experience the fear and homesickness he felt when he got off that bus from Tennessee in 1943. Months spent in indecision and an inescapable knowledge that war was only an ocean away. Thoughts you tried to keep at bay during the night took away the only rest available to recruits.

Just over thirty years later, Keesler Air Force Base, Mississippi, was not the same Air Corps Technical School the young man had seen in '43. Keesler Field was indeed just that, a field.

A strong breeze took him back in time even as he walked to catch up to his wife and girls. He felt the same rush of breath leave his lungs as it had back then when he was gazing around the dust and mud-worn landscape of his new home for basic training. Needing contact of some kind with his family, he remembered writing a letter to his mother as soon as possible

Sept. 14, 1943

Dear Mother, Dad & Joe,

I got here alright at about 7:00 o'clock. I sure hated to leave Columbia last night but I think this place is going to be alright. I haven't found out yet if I will really like it or not. I haven't been here long enough. I haven't got my clothes or haircut yet, guess I will get that tomorrow. Mother, you can write me at this address at present; I may change it in a day or so, they say.

Love, Charles

"Silence in the face of evil is itself evil: God will not hold us guiltless. Not to speak is to speak. Not to act is to act."
-Dietrich Bonhoeffer

"This old war is really bad, sometimes I don't see why God lets such things happen."
- Charles Poag

1943

1

Mississippi

Boys, not yet men, have been stepping off a bus for years with anticipation, and sometimes dread, of the military training awaiting them. For most, words like patriotism and duty were commonplace during the tumultuous times of the early 40s and the war. Being homesick and scared was not a feeling they had experienced in their short lives.

Such was the case for Charles, twenty-one years old, from Armour, a small town in Tennessee, as he stepped off the bus at Keesler Field, Mississippi. Signing up for the chance to serve his country and become a pilot, a lifelong dream, he was dressed in his Sunday best with new shoes. The first time away from home, Charles had worked at Vultee, an aircraft assembly plant in Nashville, before signing with the Army Air Corps. He didn't want to make planes; he wanted to fly them. Charles looked around the expanse of barracks, tents, and soldiers. Soldiers everywhere, marching, in line for something, talking in groups. Few looked older than he, except for those that were barking orders. Shades of black and white skin were seen; Charles had heard several thousand African Americans were stationed at Keesler in the aviation fields.

The man in uniform that met the bus didn't seem too harsh. He barely looked up from his clipboard, ticking off names as he read them off. When Charles' name was called, he nodded, then realized that he needed to speak. "Yes, here, yessir. Here, sir." The man reading from the list never raised his eyes; he just continued down the list. Following directions, the men from Charles' bus were given basic instructions for the night; and told they would receive everything they needed the next morning, promptly at 5:00 AM.

Homesickness set in quickly as Charles began preparing his cot for the night ahead. He missed his family, and he missed Louise. She occupied his thoughts most of the time, it seemed. She was the one; he was sure of it. And he owed Avery Green one hundred dollars. That might be a long time coming, but he owed him. Avery had told him he wanted to introduce him to this girl who worked at Vultee as a secretary. He promised he would like her and told him, "Her name's Louise Ramsay; she graduated from DuPont High School. Hey, she was a cheerleader, just your type! If you like her, Charles Poag, you owe me one hundred dollars. Remember that!" He had laughed and winked at the other men standing around. "Ya'll are witnesses, now! He's gonna take to her; you watch." The blind date was set up.

Avery Green was right. Charles did take to her. He was crazy about her. A letter to her and a letter to mom. Yeah, he needed to write letters and get some sleep. It was going to be an early morning.

Love, Charles

Sept. 16, 1943

Dear Mother, Dad and Joe,

We spent the first night in barracks but yesterday they moved us out to tents, six men to a tent. We sleep on cots and the floors are sand. It seems like I have been sleeping on sand for the last 3 nights. I guess you will think my clothes are really in a mess but I can't take care of them in this tent.

It started raining last night and has rained all day, this tent leaks and I liked to have drowned this morning going to breakfast. I look so funny in these GI clothes. I laugh at myself sometimes.

We haven't got all of our clothes yet. Mother, I think I am going to have to have my other shoes; these I wore have already worn blisters on my toes. So in about a week you can send them to me. You do not need to have any heels or soles put on them for I will have that done when they wear out.

I guess I will like this place ok. I sure do feel lonesome. I miss being able to come home and seeing Louise. I guess I will get over that after a while.

Mother, be sure to write all the birthdays down and send me. Also send me Dalcomb's address, Sarah's address, and Aunt Freddie's. I may have time to write them some time.

Tell Dad to take care of hisself for I know how it feels to be out in the rain all day. Tell Joe to be careful.

Love, Charles

P.S. We don't have a light in our tent so I have to stop writing when it gets dark.

World War II

Americans stay glued to news of the war across the ocean. The wars in Europe and Asia had been a topic of conversation before the attack on Pearl Harbor, but with the declaration of war by President Roosevelt on December 8, '41, families across the nation followed the latest reports. After Hitler declared war on the United States a few days later, Roosevelt declared war on Germany and Italy. The months following had been riddled with disappointments and fear, expectations and victories.

September of '43 brought cheers to the barracks across the nation as Italy surrendered. Still, families of the newest recruits were reminded of the lives lost, so many reported as killed or missing, injured or captured. Fear and grief encircled family dinner tables of homes with sons, husbands, brothers, and friends in service to their country overseas or training to join the battle.

2

Mississippi

Charles' brother Dalcomb had also signed up, and although Charles and Dalcomb weren't stationed together, their mother kept them updated on the other's whereabouts. Little brother Joe was at home, and both brothers offered advice to their younger sibling, sometimes unwanted and mostly threatening him with a beating if he didn't do as he was told. Jokingly, of course. The only girl besides his mother in the family, his sister Sarah was married and lived hours away.

It's incredibly lonely when you arrive for basic training, especially if there's no one there you know. For Charles, there was no one. Close quarters in the tent lent itself to friendship; few men arrived knowing anyone. With six men in a tent, it was close quarters. Cots were only a foot apart, and you had little choice but to make acquaintances. Charles and Frank Liston from 'just up the road apiece' in Vicksburg had little in common yet found camaraderie in their joint loneliness. Frank didn't have much family; his father had passed, leaving only him and his mother. He was a youngster compared to Charles, having just graduated from his town high school. Charles became mildly agitated when Frank would make crass remarks about Louise, and Charles tried to laugh it off, realizing that Frank was still a kid. Charles told himself that he was not going to discuss personal stuff. That he shared kisses with the prettiest girl in the world wasn't something he would talk to anybody about. Besides that, he and Frank got along very well. Charles had to make allowances for his young age, after all.

The highlight of the day the following Monday was mail call. Finally, a letter from his mother and a letter from Louise. Reading and writing letters at night was about all he could do; Frank would be snoring, sometimes annoyingly loud, while Charles finished up his letters and dropped onto the cot, exhausted. He wasn't terribly lonely any longer. He made friends. Still, lovesick and homesick. He guessed that wouldn't ever go away.

Monday night
September 20, 1943

Dear Mother, Dad, & Joe,

I got my first letter in the Army today from you. I sure was glad to hear from you. It makes you feel pretty good to think somebody is thinking about you all the time.

I am still living in a tent; I have had a pretty bad cold, but it is much better today. I think I can make it now. (I was kindly in doubt at first.)

You have to line up for everything – to go eat, to go to the toilet, to get your mail and everybody is your boss. Most of these boys are about 18 years old. I feel like a old man here – most of the fellows my age are married.

Tell Joe I said for him to take care of himself and for him to go to church, and join the church before I get back home or I will whip heck out of him.

Love, Charles

Mother, don't worry about me. I guess this army life will be ok. If I don't like it, I will tell you.

Love, Charles

Charles smiled to himself as he licked the envelope to seal the letter. It was his mother, after all. Anything he said, sounding even remotely like he was upset, would keep her up all night. There were some things, he had realized, that it was better to wait until you could talk in person. Even then, it would be wise to consider his words carefully. He yearned for that time when he could talk to his mother about everything. Staring at the top of the tent, the material moving slightly in the light wind outside, he thought about his family.

Charles worried about them, probably as much as they worried about him and Dalcomb. The war was far away, but news reports contained information about what was happening at the front. He tried not to think about it. Charles wanted to fly; the thought of taking that little Cub up in the air filled him with pride. Mother didn't understand. He thought Dad understood somewhat, and Joe knew how much his brother wanted it. Dalcomb knew; he laughed about it and made fun of him sometimes, but he wanted the same. Maybe not as much as Charles, but he wanted the same thing – to fly.

Louise knew. She worried about him; told him she prayed every day for his safety. She didn't tell him she wished he wouldn't fly and he wouldn't have to go up into that big sky with all those dangerous other planes. Louise knew how much he wanted it, so she wanted him to do it. She loved him. He loved her. That was a whole different kind of feeling. He sure hoped that they could work out this marrying thing soon. At least he was able to talk to her the night before. He sure did miss her. He closed his eyes.

Sleep came easily; the days were busy and crammed with something to do, a line to stand in, something to clean; there was little free time.

Charles and Frank seemed to have the same duties, so it made for better days when you had someone to talk to. The fall of 1943 was rainy for southern Mississippi, but no one seemed to care if you had to stand in line with the droplets running down your face. Days were spent in marching drills, more physical examinations, and even more mental tests.

Charles and Frank would discuss these tests, laughing about what the strange men administering the tests were thinking. Some of the questions seemed ridiculous and didn't make much sense. Frank said he supposed there were some crazy people there, and he didn't want to be in the Army with crazy people. Charles laughed and told him he was the crazy one; maybe he should kick him out of the tent.

September 23, 1943
Thursday

Dear Mother, Dad & Joe,

I started my physical examination today, they give us one like the one I had in Nashville. But maybe it is a little tougher than the first one. We will finish it tomorrow – I sure hope I pass it. I would hate to get washed out before I even get started. We also have to take more mental tests, too.

Mother, I have only gotten one letter from you, but I get one from Louise every day. These letters sure make you feel better when you get letters from home. I called Louise tonight and talked to her for a while so I guess she will write you before long and tell you how I am doing. I think she is a swell girl.

Mother, I get lonesome sometimes but I just say a prayer and it always helps. I hope you don't worry about me and

Love, Charles

Dalcomb for we are getting along just fine. I think this army life will be good for us both and there isn't a thing to worry about. (I haven't even come close to getting hurt yet.)

Tell Dad to write me some time. Also Joe, I know he can write if he isn't going out too much.

Love, Charles

October 2, 1943

Dear Mother, Dad & Joe,

Yesterday I was on KP. I had to run the dishwashing machine. I washed all the dishes for over 3000 men and after each meal we had to scrub the floors and walls and everything in the room. By the time we got through scrubbing we had to start washing dishes again. We started yesterday morning at 2:30 AM and worked until 9:00 last night. I sure was tired, it was the hardest I have worked in 5 years. I sure am sore this morning.

We went on review this morning. We did pretty good. There was about 100 men that fell out but that didn't bother me half as much as K.P.

We got paid Thursday. I drew $30.00. But next month I won't draw quite that much, I will have two months of insurance, and $3.75 for war bonds coming out.

Mother, it isn't anything to send dad for his birthday down here. So you go buy him a shirt and I will send you the money back.

Has Joe sold the old Ford yet? Tell him to be careful.

Tell Dad to take it easy. I think him getting put on a salary is better than working by the hour. If it is a little cut, I think that is pretty good money for a man on salary.

Love, Charles

A few weeks can seem like months when you're waiting. Waiting for something to change, for the weather to change, for the daily chores to change. Following orders became second nature to the young men waiting in the soaking rain that fell whether they were standing at attention in line, marching, or huddled inside tents with leaks and mosquitos. Waiting for the next order or the brisk snap to attention would break the monotony and usher in thoughts of the immediate work to be done instead of yearning for the comforts of home.

Charles was no different, even though he considered himself an old man compared to the other privates at Keesler. Letters from home were the highlight of any day; the weather was the downside of each day. Living in a tent for months had taken its toll on many boys. Between rain that seemed to have no end to sandstorms that blew tents down and covered the fields, there didn't seem to be an end to the discomfort. Reminding themselves that they weren't in a foxhole kept the boys both thankful and fearful. Young men may be brave, but bravery doesn't cancel out fear.

Shipping orders finally came for Charles. He and Frank received their orders on the same day and hoped that it meant they would be going to the same place. The Army is fickle sometimes; they will tell you they're shipping you out, but not where you're going.

"Can you believe it?" Frank shook his head, holding his shipping orders in the air. "Off we go, and we don't know where. Can't even write anybody and tell em, huh? And no mention of a day off for nothing, not a thing." Lying down on his cot, he stared at the ceiling.

Love, Charles

Charles didn't know how to respond. He wasn't happy about it, either, but they were going somewhere else at last. He had even written his mom and told her that this place was miserable, a letter he regretted sending. He shouldn't upset her, and that probably did the trick. For all his constant reassuring everyone that he was doing great, getting strong, and looking forward to shipping out, he had broken and told all. He knew he would have to make sure and make the next letter sound better and leave out the real emotional upheaval that pervaded every tent, every barrack.

World War II

The trainees were well-aware of what was happening on the other side of the world, at times more than the general public of the United States due to the relayed information from trainers and officers. Celebrating the heroic efforts and accomplishments of General Eisenhower and General Patton, the last months of 1943 turned attention to the skies and the 'Flying Fortresses' of the United States Army Air Forces. While the British RAF led the command, the United States had over three hundred bombers participating. Many bomber pilots perished at the hands of the superior German fighters, both from Great Britain and the United States, and it would be several months, during the spring of 1944, that the P-51 Mustang, a long-range fighter with more precise bombing tactics, would turn the tide of the air battle.

Anger and frustration grew among the recruits awaiting their turn not only in the skies but in u-boats and ground forces alike. The pilot trainees were well-versed in the accomplishments of the Red Baron, Baron Manfred von Richtofen, and though none had taken his place in the German forces for the wars fought now, the memories lingered of the exploits of the German fighters of World War I.

Families of the men fighting and training to fight both dreaded and anticipated news of the war. Fearful of the war knocking on their front door with a telegram, families huddled around the radio for the latest reports.

October 13, 1943

Dear Mother, Dad and Joe,

Well, Mother, it is raining so we can take exercise and I have a few extra minutes. Boy they sure do work us all the time, we don't have time for anything, not even time to write much. We had our other shots today and they didn't hurt me much. I just got a letter from you, also one from Sarah. I sure do like to get letters from home. I think I enjoyed that letter from Dad as well as any I have received.

I don't want you to spend your money for those sunglasses. I don't think I will need them now for a while. Sometime when you have time I would like for you to make me some cake or candy or anything to eat and send it to me about Nov. 7 for my birthday. That is all I want. Avery Green's wife sent me a box of candy last week. It sure was good. I think they sure are nice people.

Mother, I sure am glad you and Dad went to church Sunday. And I am glad Dalcomb is going. I knew he was a good boy. I sure do love him and Sarah and my whole family. They are the sweetest in the world. I am trying to live right myself. I don't drink, I never did and I try to do the best I can otherwise.

Love, Charles

Tricia Cundiff

3

Minnesota

Frank looked over Charles' shoulder as he started the letter to his mother. Charles waited until Frank was busy doing something else before he wrote to Louise because those letters were more personal, and Charles didn't want to invite Frank to kid him about his words to his girl. He had told his roommate that he and Louise had been talking about marriage which brought on a barrel of reasons from Frank why he shouldn't get married. Charles told him she wanted to marry him as much as he wanted to marry her. However, Charles' mom didn't know that. Like some things, it was better to wait until the last minute, maybe.

"Not gonna tell your mom where we're going next, huh?" Frank read the first few lines, noticed it was to Charles' mom, and lost interest, sitting on the bed across the tiny room.

Charles looked over at him, his pencil still on the paper. "Nah, no reason to do that right now. I'll tell her later. I'm gonna tell her what a great place this is; try to keep her from worrying."

"We don't know that it's all that great," Frank said, throwing a ball up against the ceiling and catching it in the opposite hand. "It might be a dump, you know. We haven't seen it all, just a bunch of cows and pigs. Yuk."

"The room's good," Charles replied, shrugging.

St. John's University, outside of St. Cloud, Minnesota, sat on 2200 acres of beautiful countryside, with the Catholic-run college a perfect location for livestock. It included several lakes, wetlands, and an extensive pine and hardwood forest. The small Catholic university had been quickly converted in preparation for the first class and was running smoothly when Charles arrived. The first Army Air Corps cadets had arrived in March of 1943, only a few months before Charles and Frank arrived. The 87th College Training Detachment at St. John's put the cadets through intensive months of training, both physical and academic. Professors of English, history, geography, mathematics, physics, and first aid were courses that had to be completed quickly; at least a year's worth of class time was done in two to five months. St. Benet's Hall had been transformed for the cadets; the kitchen staff prepared excellent meals, and the professors were acclimated to intensified classes.

The physical training included obstacle courses, workouts in the gym, and outside on skates. Temperatures reached below zero on many days, but the cadets would come in from a long march and run through the countryside with sweat dripping from their brows.

Although mentally and physically draining, the cadets adapted quickly to the rigorous training. It wasn't easy, but they were training to be pilots, and that opportunity made the time go by much faster. Running up and down the roads around the building, student officers would lead the group of cadets in song, the men's deep breathing spitting out "I've Been Workin' on the Railroad" and "The Air Corps Song." Complaints were few, and most were acknowledged with a grin.

Love, Charles

Nov. 4, 1943
Thursday afternoon

Dear Mother, Dad & Joe,

I am now in Minnesota about 200 miles from Canada. I am at St. Johns University; it is one of the prettiest colleges I have ever seen. It has 2200 acres of land for a campus. Their have their own cows and pigs and we have milk three times a day. The food is wonderful. We had steak, potatoes, milk and bread with butter, gravy and ice cream for dinner last night. Mother, this is a catholic school and the teachers all wear long robes. They say it gets 30 below zero up here and it snows six feet deep. I guess I will freeze! My new address is A/S Charles H. Poag, 87th College Training Detachment, St. John's University, Collegeville, Minnesota. Mother, it is only a few cadets up here so we get the best of everything!

Love, Charles

Nov. 6, 1943
Saturday night

Dear Mother, Dad & Joe,

I am still just laying around doing nothing. We can't get out of school to go to town for 12 days. Then we get out every Saturday night until 1:00 AM, and off all day Sunday until 8:00 p.m. Sunday night. All the cadets have rooms, 2 or 3 men per room, in St. Benet's Hall. They really feed us good, we have sweet milk three times a day and also plenty of good meat. This school is such a change from living in tents at Keesler Field that it seems wonderful to me. We have to wear our class A uniforms all the time, we have to keep our clothes pressed, our shoes shined and haircut once every week. We start to school on Monday; I don't guess I will have much time to write after then. We have about ten books and I believe they are really going to be hard.

Sunday morning

I didn't get to finish this letter last night so I will finish it today. Mother, today is November 7. I am 22 years old, I guess I am almost grown now, don't you? Don't worry about me. This is a really nice place and the food is plenty good. It is a hundred times better than Keesler Field.

Love Charles

Days were filled to the limit with classes, duties, and drills. The extreme cold would bring the young men to class shivering, full of morning meals but not enough sleep. Charles looked to the mail call as a distraction from the monotony of the days. Late night was the only time for letter writing and Charles to reread and savor the words from his fiancé in the daily letters he received.

"I've got to get me a girl," Frank said, grinning at Charles as he watched him read the latest letter from Louise. "So, I can get all gooey-eyed like you," Frank continued.

Charles glanced up from his letter and shook his head at Frank. "Don't know any girl that would have you," he responded, ducking when Frank threw his pillow across the few feet between bunks.

"What? This great specimen of a soldier?" Frank flexed his arm muscles, punching at his bicep.

Charles nodded. "Sure, man, but then you open your mouth. What comes out will make her run for the hills."

"You talking about my accent? You've got almost the same one, Charley, my man. Don't you know? These frozen girls up here love that southern talk. You wait. Saturday night, that's the night. You coming with me, right? The dance at the canteen?" Frank pulled his legs up in his bunk and laid back, staring at the ceiling.

Charles looked over at his friend. Loneliness and training together had made them friends, as distance from family and familiarity can do. Frank had finally let up on his probing questions about his relationship with Louise. Charles supposed that Frank had finally realized that Louise was permanent, not a fling, not just a girl back home that he didn't plan on seeing again. Louise was the one. He sighed with the pleasure of knowing it. Good old Avery. He had to remember to send him his hundred dollars one day. Charles would send him much more if he had it.

Charles placed the letter from Louise on the small desk in the room, carefully folded and saved. "Make you a deal, buddy. I'll go with you to the dance, help you check out the ice princesses that must live up here, and then you go to church with me Sunday morning."

Frank turned his head toward Charles and rolled his eyes. "Okay, okay. I'm not a churchy person, you know. Haven't been in years. Momma didn't put much stock in it after Pop up and died on us. I reckon the last time I was in church was right before they buried him. But yeah, if it'll get you out on the dance floor, I'll hobble in there one time."

"Hey! I didn't say anything about getting out on the dance floor!" Charles laughed.

"Aw, come on. You can give some of those old ladies a kick. I bet you can do a mean fox trot, huh?"

Charles looked at Frank, shaking his head. "I'm more of a barn dancer, to be honest. Well, maybe not. We'll see." He grinned. "Would love to be dancing with Louise, but I suppose I can pretend. What is it? Uh, swing, right? Yeah, I can do that."

"This, I've got to see," Frank said, standing up and dancing across the floor. "I'm the maestro, you know? Bring it on. The jitterbug? Man, I am king of the jitterbug. The girls will be lining up to make me their king."

"So maybe I'll just sit and keep the girls in line company while they wait for you," Charles said, laughing.

Nov. 1943

Dear Mother, Dad & Joe,

I like this place fine. We have a protestant chaplain here for the soldiers that aren't catholic, and we get to go to town on Sunday to go to church.

I don't think I will get sick here much. It is cold all the time here and at Keesler is was cold at night and hot during the day. Mother, I don't want you and Dad to worry about me. I am alright and I don't think anything will happen to me. I want you to take care of yourselves mostly. Me and Dalcomb are in the best places the Army can put a man.

I went to town on Saturday night; it is a real nice town (St. Cloud). The people are really nice to soldiers, there is only about 600 soldiers around here anywhere so the town is not overrun with soldiers like it is down there. They have a canteen in town and they serve free coffee and cake. Also there is a dance nearly every Saturday night.

I want you to quit worrying about me. I think this air corp is the safest, best branch of service I could be in. I really want to fly. This schooling is really good for me and I am getting in much better shape physically. When this war is over we will be able to get a place to live and you will live on my estate when I get a million dollars (Ha!).

Dad, I guess you have got those hogs killed by now. I wish I could have helped you. Dad, don't work too hard and stay

Love, Charles

out of that cold weather all you can. Why don't you write me again some time. You would like this town. They have bars every other door and whiskey really cheap.

Love, Charles

P.S. Tell Joe to write and take care of himself.

Tricia Cundiff

4

Minnesota

"You've been mooning over this girl for two weeks now, buddy. This ain't no place to start up something. What did you expect?" Charles shook his head as he stared at Frank.

Frank was not the one kidding him anymore about Louise. Once he had looked into the eyes of that Minnesota farm girl from a little village just down the road from St. John's, Frank Liston was smitten. Charles had to bite his tongue several times, remembering how Frank had kidded him about Louise. He's still just a kid, Charles would have to remind himself.

Frank had not let Charles off the hook; he had attended the dance with Frank and spent most of the night entertaining the elderly ladies posing as chaperones for the youngest of the girls. Charles wasn't particularly interested in the young women attending the dance, his heart belonged to Louise, and she was in his thoughts as he had watched the young men and women play their coy and flirtatious games with each other.

Charles was more inclined to nod politely to the older women sitting on the sidelines of the dance floor, listening as they continued their litany of what young folks should and shouldn't be wearing and the horrors of war on the other side of the world. Keeping one ear attuned to any news he was unaware of, he did enjoy their banter; it reminded him of his mother and her conversations with her friends.

Frank's dancing form would glide by his line of sight frequently, and he had been surprised to note that Frank's partner stayed the same almost from the minute they had entered the room. Most of the men there – Charles had to remind himself that they were men, although more often than not, they seemed like boys – wore their uniforms, ill-fitting though they might be. He looked down at his uniform, noting it fit better than before. The physical drills and exercise had done their due diligence, and he felt stronger, though heavier than ever. The men – and boys – dancing were the same or would be, given enough time. Time. Time was something that preyed on the minds of most of the cadets at the dance and probably most of the others in attendance also. Concentrating on how time seemed to stand still during war-torn eras, Charles suddenly broke out in a sweat and had to leave the dance, raising eyebrows as he hurried out the door. Time. Time enough to love and laugh. Time to marry, to have a baby with Louise. Time to see his mother and dad again, to joke and kid around with his brothers. Time was even more precious when it looked as fleeting as it did now.

Sitting in their room only a couple of weeks after the dance, the concept of time continued to occupy Charles' thoughts. Sometimes it seemed to pass by so quickly, and others, well, the hours crept by so slowly that he ached inside for the next part of his life to begin.

Charles closed his eyes as he waited for Frank to begin again on his litany of reasons that he needed to see Sherry again, his new love. But Charles' thoughts were never far from what was going on across the ocean, in war-torn areas of the world that he had yet to see.

New reports were frequent, with journalists reporting on battles won and lost. Ernie Pyle, that brave reporter that dared all, painted pictures with his words that tore at the heartstrings of young and old men and women alike. A few newspapers were passed among the cadets, but they were usually a few days old before they made their way to Charles. Most of the reports in the papers were old news by the time they reached St. John's. Charles knew there was much not reported, kept secret and away from the public, and he appreciated the need for it in wartime. There was enough blared from the radio and reported in the newspapers to keep anyone interested aware of the war events and casualties, along with the wins and losses.

Every cadet, every soldier, dealt with the fear. Though they might not admit it, not even to themselves, Charles knew it existed. He told himself that it is natural, human nature, to fear the unknown. And to a soldier, especially one in the field, every day is an unknown.

Charles wanted to fly. He didn't let himself dwell too long on his purpose for the flight; the pilot's job was to fly. Turning his head toward Frank, he saw him still staring at the ceiling, thinking what? Did he wonder about flying? Did he think about engaging in combat with one of those German fighters, and what could happen? Did he think about what he had back home? Charles smiled. Frank's mind was on one thing and one thing only. Sherry.

"What you staring at, man?"

Charles' meanderings halted as Frank's voice cut into his thoughts. "Just thinking, that's all," Charles said, grinning back at Frank. "I remember seeing you dance past me while I was sitting over on the side with the old ladies, and I wondered how come you were with the same little chickadee every time."

"Don't call her that, "Frank said, huffing as he sat up on the bunk. "She just got me, man, that's all. It was like, aw, you know, like she already knew me and was waiting for me. She even said that, Charley, 'I've been waiting for you,' she said. I couldn't believe my luck. She was the prettiest one there, wasn't she, Charley? She was."

"She won't win a contest with Louise, but yeah, she's pretty. A lot better looking than you are, that's for sure. The pickings must be awfully bad if she's been waiting on you," Charles said, grinning at the lovestruck face of his friend.

"You're prejudiced. To you, nobody is as pretty as your girl. I've seen you stare at that picture with your silly grin. Louise is pretty. Sherry is, is, is, well, darn it, she's special," Frank said, shrugging.

"That's how it's supposed to be, I guess. You're falling for her hard, Frank. Maybe back up a little. Two weeks. That's all it's been. Two weeks. You've seen her, what, three times? I've known Louise a lot longer." Charles looked at his friend. He was worried about him. Charles didn't know Sherry; he had hardly even talked to her. Frank had introduced her, but they hadn't really talked. She seemed young; that was about all Charles noticed besides, yes, she was a knock-out beauty. Still, no competition for his Louise.

"Yeah? You've known Louise a lot longer. So? How long did it take you to know she was the one?" Frank questioned.

Charles nodded. Frank had him there. "You're right. I knew pretty quickly. Right off the start, I guess. Maybe it just took a while for me to say it out loud."

"You're just not much for talking, are you? Well, I am. I talk a lot, I know. But I mean what I say, and Sherry's the one. I'm going to marry this girl before we leave Minnesota. She's coming with me." Frank nodded his head.

Charles held up his hands. "Whoa, buddy. Marry her? Holy mackerel! You take a girl on the dance floor, cut a rug, and get married? Slow it down; you're not on the beam, Frank."

Frank stared at Charles. A long silence, and then "That's funny coming from you, Charley-boy. You've been talking about getting married since you got here. Heck, since I met you at

Keesler. No right to talk, cadet. No way to talk at all." Frank got up and walked out, slamming the door as he left.

Maybe I didn't handle that very well, Charles thought. He wished he could talk to Louise. She would know the right thing to say. He felt much older than Frank, although he was only a few years his senior. But the thing with him and Louise, it was different. They were, well, they were real. Did Frank feel that way? He couldn't, could he? Charles laughed at himself. Yeah, he guessed he was too hard on Frank. One minute he was thinking about dying and not getting to spend a life with Louise, and the next minute he told his friend that he was nuts. Did he miss the part in church about do unto others? Okay, maybe it was time for a bit of prayer. Or maybe a lot of it. Right after he finished his letter to Louise and wrote one to his mother.

November 1943

Dear Mother, Dad & Joe,

I guess you have got those hogs killed by now. I wish I could have helped you.

I found out that I was going to be sent to California for classification. I will also get my flying out there or maybe in Texas. I think I will like it in California and I will only be out there about 6 months until I can finish this course and get my wings. Then I will probably be sent back east for the rest of my training. Everybody that leaves this school has to go to Santa Anna, California. That is pretty close to Hollywood. They may make a movie star out of me when I get there. I will still be here about 3 to 4 months before I go to California.

Tricia Cundiff

Mother, if I hear about you and Daddy worrying about me I am going to be mad because I am really enjoying this training and I am getting in better shape physically than I have been in a long time. I am getting to do a lot of traveling and seeing the country. Don't worry, I am going to be alright.

Love, Charles

Love, Charles

World War II

News of the War across the ocean invaded every aspect of daily life in America, especially in those homes with soldiers fighting and those training to aid in the fight. Americans could subscribe to morning and evening newspapers, and many mothers, fathers, wives, and children stayed glued to their radio for news of battles won and lost. Not all losses were on the war front, however.

The training of airmen, although not publicized, was dangerous because it involved old aircraft and inexperienced recruits. By the end of World War II, over 8000 men were killed in training accidents or other aircraft tragedies. As news of the loss of another son would trickle through the grapevine of voices in small cities and towns across the country, mothers would weep and worry.

The Poag household was no different. The Columbia Mule Day Celebration, held again in 1943 after the parade's absence in 1942 due to the war, did little to lift the spirits of Charles' parents and his brother, Joe. A few miles down the road from Armour, Columbia had officially celebrated Mule Day since 1934. The county-fair-like day had always provided entertainment for the whole family, bringing in relatives and friends from neighboring towns. However, this one proved different, with news of the fighting continuing on foreign soil and the loss of human life increasing in horrific numbers. As people lined the street waiting for the parade, talk consisted of hushed conversations involving who had lost someone and whose sons remained overseas. Families in and around Columbia, Tennessee were no different than those across America, dreading the knock at the door, hating to listen to the news, but dependent upon it for any morsel of news from the front.

Although Charles and Dalcomb had yet to enter the frays of war across the ocean, fear and prayer consumed their mother and father, while pride in their sons led to flags placed in windows for all to see from outside. Young Joe, waiting his turn to enlist, wanted to join his brothers in their bravery and patriotism despite his mother's tears.

The fall of 1943 had brought news of the surrender of Italy, but the continued attacks of the Allies' movement to Rome in October and November were slow. The number of fatalities and injuries grew, and America waited for good news.

5

Minnesota

Nov. 25, 1943, Thursday

Dear Mother, Daddy, Sarah & Joe,

I received yours and Sarah's letter today. I was glad to hear that Sarah is home with you. I am glad Mike got a job in New Orleans. I guess maybe that company will last a long time. Well, today is Thanksgiving. I guess we all have plenty to be thankful for. I tried to find some thanksgiving cards but they didn't have any up here. I guess this time next year, this war will be over. I honestly believe it will be.

I am sending our menu for dinner today, it was really good. We only got out of classes for one hour after dinner. So I just thought I would write you and Louise and send you our menus so you will know I am not starving, in fact gaining weight.

Love, Charles

Charles sat back in his chair and looked over at Frank. "Here. My letter to Mother. Don't you want to read it?" Any other time Frank would be looking over his shoulder, checking to see if Charles had said anything to his mother about Louise. Not this time. Frank lay on his bunk, sullen and quiet.

Frank reached out and took the one-page letter Charles handed to him. Reading it silently, he didn't say anything until he handed it back to Charles. "Who's Sarah?"

"My sister, you know, married to Mike?"

"So why is she living with your mom? Trouble in love, huh?"

"Nah, nothing like that. She's going to have a baby, and you know, just stuff, I guess." Charles looked at Frank, noticing that he wasn't paying attention. "What's up, Frank?"

Standing up and stretching, Frank shook his head. "Not a thing, Charley-boy. Not a thing."

"Heard from your mom?" Charles asked, hoping the answer was yes. Frank didn't get many letters; when he did, they were short, and he didn't share the contents. Though Frank felt comfortable prying and asking questions, Charles was more hesitant, maybe because he was pretty sure that Frank's letters wouldn't be anything like those he received from his mother. Frank would hang onto every word if Charles read them aloud and happily read them himself if offered. Charles spent an hour explaining the process of killing hogs to Frank when it was mentioned in a letter from home.

"Yeah, she's fine, my mom, she's fine. Got herself a beau, I guess. That's all she writes about. Some old geezer, a real drip, you know." Frank straightened his bunk, not looking at Charles.

"How do you know he's a bore? Have you met him?" Charles pushed just a little. Frank could talk a blue streak but didn't offer much about himself.

"Nope, don't need to. Same as the others. They're all the same." Dismissing the subject, he nodded at Charles. "Come on; we've got to get back to class. Thanksgiving or not, they want us back in class in less than five." He patted his stomach. "I could go for a nap after all that food. But nope. Let's go, man, let's go!"

"Okay, okay. Whew. Yeah, I'm stuffed myself. I didn't know it was so late. I thought you were going to try and call Sherry. Did you talk to her?" One phone was in the building, and sometimes the line was long.

Frank shrugged. "Nah, I'll try later on, maybe. Saturday night, I'll see her then. She'll be there."

Charles guessed that Frank had not talked to Sherry since Sunday. As he and Frank walked from the bus stop to the movie theater, they ran into Sherry and her parents leaving the night service at church. Introductions were made. Sherry's parents seemed pleasant and were kind, asking about their families and expressing concern over their anticipation of joining the war effort overseas.

Frank wanted to ask Sherry to attend the movie with him and tried to catch her eye, but she and her parents left quickly, and Frank had not talked to her since then.

"Coming, slowpoke?" Frank tapped his finger on the doorframe.

Charles nodded and grabbed his textbook. He didn't have time to write Louise; he would do it later.

He needed to read her letter again; maybe it would help him to write back something as good as she had written to him. The woman he wanted to marry could make him smile from across the country; he wanted her to smile when she read his letter, too. Her lipstick on the bottom of the letter reminded him of her lips on his. Shaking his head, he bounded down the steps and across the snow-covered yard to the building that held classrooms.

Speeding through the textbooks to cram a year's worth of instruction into a few short months, the classes were tough. The teachers were sometimes harsh but showed compassion for the young men striving to complete their education and move on to their duties as airmen.

It was a miracle that the cadets found time for little other than studying, physical drills, eating, and sleeping, yet somehow found the resources and time to listen to the military band formed by the few young men who were musically inclined. The musicians soon became a top-notch military band, playing in parades and Saturday retreats. Jack Webb, a future Hollywood movie actor, attended the university at St. Cloud and returned to help produce a variety show featuring the band. The show sold tickets and donated twelve hundred dollars to the USO. Activities such as these were important for the morale of the cadets. All were anxious, awaiting their time to complete their classwork and move on to flying. Ten hours of Cub flying at the local St. Cloud airport would complete their assignment in St. Cloud and then on to California.

Charles was ready to place St. Cloud behind him. For many reasons.

Nov. 29, 1943
Monday night

Dear Mother, Dad and Joe and Sarah,

This is pretty nice now. I can almost write the whole family in one letter. I guess Sarah is a lot of company if she isn't much good for anything else. HaHa! Bet she can really cook good now though.

I am getting along just fine. I went ice skating Sunday afternoon. Boy you should have seen me on those skates. I fell every way in the world, but before I quit I was doing pretty good. I could skate a half mile without falling. Ice skating isn't half as hard as I thought it was. The only thing is that it is pretty hard on your ankles. I was plenty sore this morning, but they got that out during P.T. today.

I didn't go to town Sunday, I had to stay here and study. We had four tests today so I had to study so I could pass. I am doing pretty good in Math and Physics and Geography. But that English and History is giving me heck. I haven't failed anything yet. I had an average of 95 in Math, 92 in Physics last week, that's pretty good.

Tell Dad that Saturday we had to trot five miles. I made it but it liked to have killed me. It was five degrees above zero and I had on a sweat shirt under my GI clothes and I sweated all the way through both uniforms cold as it was. Out of 300 men who started only about 55 of us made it back in without having to stop and walk in.

Love, Charles

Thursday night, Dec. 2, 1943

Dear Mother, Dad, Sarah & Joe,

Well, we have guard duty tonight for 24 hours. We just finished guard duty in our course in school, so every time a class finishes the course they have guard duty for one day. I have to go on duty at 9:30 pm and stay on two hours. We have two hours on duty and four hours off for 24 hours. It sure is cold out there now. It is about zero degrees now and will probably be five below before morning. I have all the clothes I own on and I guess I will stay plenty warm. They issued us hoods to wear the other day. They are made out of wool just like a sweater and they cover your head and face, all except your eyes and come down under your coat. They sure keep your head and neck warm but you look like something from Mars with them on.

Mother I am glad Louise came down to see you. I think she is a sweet girl and I intend to marry her as soon as I can get to making enough money to keep her up!

Love, Charles

Charles sealed the envelope and sat back in the chair. It was late, and he was tired, but his thoughts were on Louise and getting married. His mother knew how he felt about Louise and must have guessed that he planned to marry her. He and Louise were talking about it; so much depended on where he was stationed and what they could afford. Louise liked all his family, but she knew his mother would be the one she needed to impress. He couldn't imagine that she had not already done that.

Charles thought about why he hesitated to reassure his mother about Louise. He didn't want her to worry about him and whether he could take care of a wife. He needed to let her know that he and Louise would be working; they would help each other. Louise was wonderful; she would be the most supportive partner a man could hope for. He supposed mothers everywhere felt the same way about their children. He remembered how she worried about Sarah getting married, as did the whole family. Not really worried, Charles guessed, more like protective. Sarah was the only girl and even if she was older, her brothers wanted to make sure that this Mike Cannon guy she wanted measured up. So far, so good. He was a good guy, and Sarah really loved him.

Smiling to himself, he closed his eyes. He could see her, his Louise, and he longed to hold her again.

Some things you couldn't talk to your mother about.

Frank walked into the room and threw his coat on his cot, blowing in his hands. "Colder than a witches' – uh, you know – out there."

"What were you doing out there anyway?" Charles shook his head. "We've got to be up earlier than usual tomorrow."

Frank just shrugged and started peeling off clothes, pulling the covers back on his bunk. "Just a little jog around the building."

Charles figured Frank had been in line for the phone. If he had talked to Sherry, he would have said so. Sherry had not shown up at the Saturday dance, and Frank had come home early, quiet and brooding. Charles tried to talk to him, but Frank wasn't responsive. Treading carefully around the subject, Charles had left Frank to figure it out himself.

Turning out the lamp at his desk, the room settled into darkness. "Uh, 'night," Charles said as he slipped under his covers.

"Yeah," was all the response Frank offered.

Charles lay in the bunk, staring at the ceiling. The wind blew through the trees outside the window. Paper-thin shades over the windows did little to keep the spotlights from St. Benet's Hall out of the rooms. The shadows of tree limbs danced across the mottled dingy ceiling, but Charles didn't notice. His prayers concerned Louise, his mother, and his friend, Frank. And the war.

Tricia Cundiff

World War II

December 7, 1943

On December 7, 1941, Japanese planes attacked the United States Naval Base at Pearl Harbor, Hawaii Territory, killing more than 2,300 Americans. The U.S.S. Arizona was destroyed, and the U.S.S. Oklahoma capsized. A total of twelve ships sank or were beached in the attack, and nine additional vessels were damaged. More than 160 aircraft were destroyed, and over 150 were damaged.

The following day, in an address to a joint session of Congress, President Franklin Roosevelt called December 7, 1941, "a date which will live in infamy." Congress declared war on Japan, abandoning the nation's isolationism policy and ushering the United States into World War II.

On December 11, 1941, three days after the United States declared war on Japan, Adolf Hitler and Nazi Germany declared war against the United States. That same day, the United States declared war on Germany and Italy.

War had raged for two years since that fateful day in 1941, and the second anniversary of the attack had brought no conclusion to the war against the Germans and Japanese. Although Italy had surrendered, ground troops were still working their way northward, and the German army still had control of Rome.

Soldiers on the front, as well as those training to join them, remembered the date and reaffirmed their determination to be a part of the men that stopped the advancement of the armies of Hitler and Hirohito.

Families of those serving in the military remained by their radios for any news, memories unbroken of the devastating news only two years before. Voices that had proclaimed the war would be short and the United States would quickly end the fighting were hushed as the war correspondents sent news of equal defeats and victories.

Training continued in the posts scattered across the United States, readying men for their part in the war, whether in the skies, on the ocean, or the ground. War raged on across the world.

Tricia Cundiff

6

Minnesota

Frank wanted to talk; Charles could tell. They had been cooped up in St. Benet's Hall for two days, only leaving for meals. Frank was drumming his fingers across the desk, staring at the wall. Charles waited. He had learned Frank's moods. I guess this is what parents go through, he thought to himself. It would be much easier to shake him until he blurted out what was happening in that thick head. But it wouldn't do any good. Then he would clam up, and there would be more glaringly silent days before he would speak again.

Finally, Frank turned to Charles. "I called her; I talked to Sherry."

"Yeah? How did that go?" Charles suspected that things were not going as well as Frank would like.

"Every time I've called, her mother or father says she's not there. This time she answered. She whispered most of the time; I guess she didn't want them to know she was talking to me. Her daddy said she couldn't talk to me anymore. She's sixteen, Charley. Just sixteen. Seventeen the first week of January, but still, he thinks she's too young." Frank talked in a monotone.

"That is pretty young," Charles ventured.

"What? Sixteen? My mom had me when she was seventeen! I know a guy right here, right now, in this hallway. They're married, and their girl was sixteen when they got married. I asked."

"Frank. You were nineteen on your birthday, right? You'll be, uh, twenty in March. You enlisted when you were eighteen; you made a choice. Would you make the exact same decisions now? Huh?" Charles waited for an answer but only received a shrug. "See? That's what I mean. You might have changed your mind if you had waited. She's young. You don't know how she might feel next year or the next."

"You're wrong. I do know. She told me. She loves me; she wants to be with me. She said I'm the best thing that's ever happened to her." Frank stood and paced around the small room.

"Shoot. You've seen her, what, three times? How could she possibly know that?" Charles laughed.

The look Frank shot at Charles stopped his laughter. Okay, he needed to remember he was not talking to a rational man right now. He was talking to a kid who thought he was in love. Or lust, probably.

"Okay, say she does love you. And you, from what I gather, think – okay, okay – you love her, too. You can't do anything foolish, man. You can't go against her father. That will just let you in for trouble. You know that." Charles knew he was grabbing at straws.

"How old is Louise? She couldn't be much older than Sherry." Frank had cooled somewhat, but he needed to talk.

"Louise will be 23 on the eleventh of January; I've got to figure out what to send her. I haven't sent anything for Christmas yet. Not that I have any money to speak of," Charles replied, focusing on what he needed to accomplish in a short amount of time.

"Twenty-three? Wow. I didn't expect that. I thought maybe nineteen like me, twenty at the most. She's a real beauty, but that's old, man – she's older than you!" Frank shook his head.

Charles couldn't help but laugh again. "Yeah, we're really old, all right. A few months older than me, we joke about that. I'm so lucky to have her, Frank. I don't mean anything talking about this to you now when you're so down about Sherry, but you've got to see what I've seen. Here I am, this regular guy, and somehow this beautiful woman had managed to avoid getting hitched to somebody else. Several wannabes tried to attach themselves to my beauty, but she didn't find the right one – until me, she says. We were meant to be together. The same for me, Frank. I thought I had found the one when I was still in high school. But it wasn't right. Somehow, God lets you know when you're walking in the right direction. There you go. He put Louise and me right on that same road. He knew. I didn't know. Louise didn't know. But He did." Charles had fallen into a reverie of his own and didn't notice that Frank had closed his eyes and laid his head between his hands.

"I can't give up on Sherry. Not yet," Frank said, leaving the room, but at least not slamming the door.

So, he's not angry, Charles thought to himself. Maybe he'll think about it. There's plenty of time for that. It's not like there's anywhere to go.

December 12, 1943
Sunday morning

Dear Mother, Dad, Sarah & Joe,

I am spending a very quiet weekend. We are quarantined and can't leave the campus on account of the flu epidemic going around up here. They won't let us go outside the building unless we have on all the clothes we have. We haven't had any PT or drill for the last couple of days.

Tricia Cundiff

Nobody has any flu here but it is all over St. Cloud and they are afraid we might catch it if we went to town. Boy, they really look out for you up here.

They issued us some flying boots the other day so we can wear them over our shoes to keep our feet warm when we go out. It sure is cold up here, but when you put on all the stuff they make you wear outside you can't even feel the cold.

Sarah, it looks like you and Mike are having a hard time. You tell Mike that I said for him to go to work and stay out of this Army as long as he can.

Tell Joe I don't guess I will be able to get him anything this Xmas. But I will let him wear my clothes so he will just have to get by on that until I have more money.

Dad, how is the news now? I hardly get to read the paper or listen to the radio at all. I believe this war will be over before long, don't you?

Love, Charles

Love, Charles

World War II

Christmas 1943

With World War II raging across the oceans and many homes absent family members, Americans in the US tried to celebrate Christmas as best they could. The gatherings were bittersweet and filled with the longing of loved ones serving on foreign soil, training on American soil to join other servicemen, or lost in the massive number of battlefield casualties.

Mothers at home with children wanted to make Christmas a happy time, but toys were scarce. Metal and rubber toys weren't available, and toymakers switched to the new plastics, cardboard, and wood to make the toys. Dolls, wooden jeeps, airplanes, and playsets made of paper and cardboard were popular toys during the war.

Travel was curtailed, so few visited family members in other towns. Gasoline was rationed and saved for necessary trips. The large Christmas dinners with many friends and relatives, a special treat each holiday season, were small compared to past years. The rationing of food items such as sugar, butter, and meat made fancy dinners impossible.

Blackout conditions for the West coast, dim-outs on the Eastern Coast, and eventually a nationwide dim-out to conserve fuel meant the Christmas season was not quite as bright as before. Christmas trees were hard to find in some areas but available to those with the men left at home who could cut down their own.

The music of Christmas during World War II would remain popular for years. Bing Crosby recorded "White Christmas" in 1942, "I'll be Home for Christmas" was a hit in 1943, and Judy Garland's "Have Yourself a Merry Little Christmas" in 1944 reminded everyone of better times and the hope for them to come again.

Christmas during World War II was heartbreaking for many, but Americans at home and across the oceans did their best to recognize and celebrate Christ's birth.

Minnesota

December 18, 1943
Saturday night

Dear Mother, Sarah and Joe,

Well, mother, it is beginning to seem like Christmas now. I have been getting a lot of Christmas cards and also presents from you and Sarah and Dad. That coconut cake was really good, so was that fruit cake. I am going to try and catch up on my writing this weekend because we are still quarantined and can't go to town. They have about 70 men in the hospital with colds or the flu. I guess I am too dumb to catch a cold or the flu because I really feel good.

Dad, I sure wish I could come home for Christmas, but I guess that would be almost impossible because we only have from Friday night until Sunday night and I wouldn't even have time to get home. I sure do appreciate you sending me that $5.00 but I am sending it back to you because I want to call up home some time during Christmas. It will cost at least $5.00 to call and we only have a pay phone up here. I will just call collect and you can pay for this call. I get by just fine on this $37.00 per month. I don't have any extra money but I have all I need. You don't have to spend much in the army.

That is about all I know for now. I have to write Dalcomb a letter so I guess I will have to stop. Tell Joe to write me again. I would like to know what kind of car he has now. And how he is getting along. He won't write as much as Daddy does. I am going to beat his ears down when I see him again (I guess that will probably be quite a while) and he will be big enough to whip me then.

I really like the Army if they would just keep me close to home.

Love, Charles

Charles looked around the room. Christmas cards he had received were taped onto the walls, the only Christmas decorations in their small space. Frank had gone outside to skate. The breaks for a little physical exercise were good for both of them. Thankfully, Frank had remained free of the sickness invading the school, and they both remained healthy. Rumors spread through the recruits that the epidemic could become as deadly as the flu epidemic of 1918, and those with any symptoms were sent immediately to the doctor. News of the illness indicated that although there were some serious consequences in England and Wales, the United States was not experiencing the same complications even though it seemed the flu epidemic originated in Minnesota.

Conversation remained strained between Charles and Frank; Charles guessed that it might improve when Frank met someone new and could forget about Sherry. He felt sorry for Frank; Charles realized how important Louise was and how she helped him look forward to something and not focus solely on the war. Hopefully, the quarantine would be lifted soon, and they could go back to town, take in a movie, something.

Few cadets could make it home for Christmas; only a couple would see their wives for a few hours over the weekend. Christmas was hard; Charles had not realized how difficult it would be. This would be the first time he had not been with his family for the holiday, the first time not attending his church for the Christmas service.

Again, he felt sorry for Frank. The holiday cards on the wall were all for him, from relatives and friends. Frank hadn't received anything from anyone for Christmas, opening the package the cadets received from the military with little enthusiasm. Mandatory attendance at the holiday service was the only reason Frank participated in any songs of the season.

Charles didn't know what he could do to help Frank, but it made him more thankful for his family and Louise. All he could do was pray for him and offer his friendship in the only way he knew. He was there for Frank, to listen and advise if asked. Most of their conversations centered around happenings in the war and where they would be stationed next. Late nights would open up whispered conversations about the horrors awaiting them when they were shipped out. The war seemed far away and yet so very close sometimes.

December 23, 1943
Thursday night

Dear Mother, Dad, Sarah and Joe,

Well, Mother, I got yours and dad's picture today and I was disappointed. In all the letters you wrote you said that the pictures were not any good. Well, the one I have is the best picture I ever saw. I think it is really good; it looks just like both of you. I believe that you both look better than you did when I left home. I sure am proud of that picture. I showed it to all the fellows. My mother and dad looks better than any of their folks. I am going to town tomorrow and I am going to buy a frame for it.

They finally will let us go to town this weekend and I think we are going to have a party Saturday night. So, I will write and tell you what kind of Christmas I had after this weekend.

Louise sent me a real nice pipe for Christmas. She also bought me one of those big suitcases to match my small one. They sure are nice. I have always wanted one but never could get ahold of enough money to buy one. I will have a nice set of luggage when I get out of this Army anyhow.

Mother, you asked me about going to church here. If I go to church on Sunday, I have to go in town at nine o'clock in the morning and stay until eight o'clock at night before I can catch the bus. I usually have to study on Sunday and I don't have time to spend all day in town. I do read my Bible every Sunday and also every chance I get through the week so you see I am still a pretty good boy. I am going to try to get to church sometime during Christmas.

Love, Charles

"No, I can't eat any more of that. It's yours, Charley. I'm not going eat your presents all up," Frank held up his hands and shook his head at Charles' offering of more fruit cake.

Charles laid the tin on the small table. "Eat all you want. Do you think I can eat all this stuff? Come on, Frank. We're all family here. We make our families in this war. And I made you in mine. Besides, you'll help me. If I eat all this stuff, I won't be able to fit into my dress uniform."

"All right. I will take some more of those cookies. Who sent these?" Frank picked out two of the cookies in a box beside the fruit cake tin.

"Sarah, I think. Or maybe Louise. I put them all in the same box; it could be either one. Louise bought some cookies and sent me; Sarah made the sugar cookies." Charles relaxed in the bunk, his hands behind his head. Glancing over at Frank, he laughed. "Please, please, eat all you want," he said as he watched his friend stuff another piece of fruit cake in his mouth.

"You said to eat it, man. I'm not going to pass this up. You've got some family back there, Charley. I hope I meet them someday and thank them for all this stuff," Frank replied, surprising Charles with his sentiment.

"You will, Frank, you will. You should come with me when we get leave. I mean, you know, if it's okay with your mom and all." Charles didn't want to remind Frank that his mother had not sent anything to him for Christmas.

Most of the young men had families longing for them to be home for Christmas and had sent food and small presents. Others, like Frank, had few family members and didn't hear from anyone back home. Another cadet had lost his parents in a house fire only two years before and had joined the Army immediately, leaving no one behind. There were stories upon stories among the young men readying themselves for combat.

December 28, 1943
Tuesday night

Dear Mother, Dad, Sarah and Joe,

I hope all of you had a good Christmas. My Christmas wasn't so good this year. I started trying to call you Christmas morning at 7:00 o'clock and tried until 7:00 pm Saturday night. Then I tried again all day Sunday and I never could get a call through until last night. I wanted to talk to you real bad last night but I couldn't hear a word you said so I didn't want to waste time talking and not being able to hear anything. I will call you again before long, maybe I can hear better the next time.

I sure was glad Dalcomb got to come home. I sure wish I could have been home. I got pretty lonesome a few times but I just thought well, maybe I can be home next Christmas and just went on. We got to go to town Friday night and stay until 12:00 pm. Then we really had a good dinner out here at school Christmas day. It sure was good. It was one of the biggest dinners I ever saw. We had a party in town Saturday night. The party was pretty good. They gave us all a present and I got this stationary. The school also gave us a sack of apples, oranges and nuts. So I guess I had a pretty good Christmas after all. I sure wish I could have seen Dalcomb. I bet he is a deal in those cadet clothes.

I went skating Sunday on the Mississippi River. It runs right through St. Cloud, and it is frozen over and you can skate all the way across it.

It sure did make me mad when I couldn't hear you on the phone last night. I am going to call again before long. I sure wanted to talk to you and Daddy both. Well, Mother, I hope it is God's will that we can all be home together next Christmas and this war is over.

Love, Charles

1944

7

World War II

    The Allies carried heavy losses and struggled to make headway in Italy due to the area's winter weather and difficult terrain. However, the slow progress against the German line did bring some good news to America. The Allies had broken through one line and worked slowly towards their target, Rome. The casualties of war continued to climb, and American families feared the worst and prayed for an end to the war and victory.

    Constant reassurances from President Roosevelt did little to calm the families that sat beside their radios, waiting for the news that the Germans and Japanese had retreated, that the time of victory was close. News traveled more quickly of lost sons and husbands across the ocean, battles lost, and the evil actions of the enemy. Patriotism was high, yet prayers were raised to end the fighting, the separation of families, and the loss of men, young and old men, on the other side of the world.

Families went about their daily chores, trying to maintain continuity in their lives while waiting and listening for any news, good or bad. In the United States, pressures mounted even as the economy boomed, as military spending increased jobs and production. The unemployment rate dropped as women filled jobs historically held by the men that were fighting in the war. But the war also disrupted trade, limiting the stock of some items. Supplies such as gasoline, butter, sugar, and canned milk were rationed because they needed to be diverted to the war effort.

Minnesota

"I got a letter from my mom," Frank laid it down on Charles' desk. "She sent me five dollars. That was a shock. I guess she got it from her new boyfriend, but she does have a new job. Oh yeah, she moved. Two months ago. Just now got around to letting me know where she is."

Charles picked up the letter offered and scanned over it. He knew this was a sore subject for his friend; while Frank watched as Charles received letters from home almost every time there was a mail call, Frank had not received anything since before Thanksgiving. He knew that Frank had tried to call home over Christmas, but he didn't think he had talked to anyone.

"She's probably having a hard time, Frank. She says she wished you could have been home for Christmas." Charles wasn't sure how to console his friend. All he could think of was how lucky he was to have a family with him in their prayers daily. How lucky he was to have his Louise.

"Yeah, well. If I had thought of surprising her and gone home, she wouldn't have been there, would she? She moved, and I didn't know." Frank spoke in a monotone, displaying little emotion.

Charles didn't respond. What was there to say?

"Going down to play some basketball. Coming?" Frank stood and stretched.

"Nah, I need to write some letters," Charles said before thinking. Rubbing it in that he had letters to write to his family seemed cruel.

"Sure thing. See you later," Frank said as he left the room.

Charles ached for his friend, but what could he do? He had written to Louise about Frank and some other guys there, but she had not offered anything other than prayers for all of them. He guessed that was all he could do.

January 2, 1944
Sunday night

Dear Mother, Dad, Sarah & Joe,

Well, I tried to call you today and they couldn't get anyone to answer the phone. I just want to say hello and wish you a happy new year.

Everything is just fine up here. We do the same thing over and over everyday so it is hard for me to find anything to write about. I went to town Saturday night and everything was closed. We had all day Saturday off and didn't have to go to school.

We had to trot 4 miles Friday. We trotted across the lake on ice and everybody was slipping down and falling all over everything.

Love, Charles

January 4, 1944
Tuesday night

Dear Mother, Dad, Sarah and Joe,

Mother, I want you to check out $50 out of the bank and send to me. I don't really need it but I had to buy some tennis shoes and PT equipment and that along with Christmas took all the extra money I had saved. I like to keep a little extra money so if anything ever comes up so I could get home. I would have enough to make the trip. I *have about $25 loaned out with good interest to the fellows here at school and I have 23 dollars left out of my pay check for this month. I like to have about $75 all the time. If I don't use it before I start making $75 per month when I get to be a cadet, I will send it back. Maybe they will pay me a little more per month. It is hard to get by on $34.00 per month and pay for your laundry and everything.*

Love, Charles

Charles sat in the canteen, pulling paper out of his back pocket. The man behind the bar loaned him a pen; he had a pencil, but he must have lost it in the movie. Movement on the stool beside him, and he turned to see Frank motioning for the man behind the counter to bring him something, pointing at Charles' drink and holding up two fingers.

"Where you been? I thought you were coming to the movie. Tarzan's Desert Mystery? You said you wanted to see it, but it will be gone next week! You missed it, man. That Johnny Weissmuller, he can do it all," Charles looked at Frank. His friend was staring straight ahead, nodding his head.

"I was there; I was just in the back. I had to, well, I was sitting with Sherry. No, no, don't look at me like that. We just had some things to say. I'm not seeing her again," Frank sipped the beer in front of him. Looking down at his glass, he glanced up at the barkeep and said, "What is this?"

The man behind the bar shrugged. "Miller, I think. Either that or Pabst. They don't send us much German stuff anymore, but that one's made here, so I 'reckon it's okay."

Frank shook his head and looked over at Charles. "That's what we got here, huh? German drinks?"

Charles grinned. "I never thought about it. But I guess if they live here, they must like it and be a good German, right? Tell me about Sherry. So, you're in the movie theater, but you're not watching Tarzan? What a waste, man!"

"First off, I didn't know there was a such thing as a good German," Frank began, and Charles shrugged.

"The bad guys are the ones that want to kill us; I can't believe that everybody in Germany wants to kill us. Just the ones that Hitler orders to do that. Just like the Japs, man. I don't know, I don't want to think that there's a whole world of people out there that are just evil," Charles picked up his glass and finished the drink that had been sitting in front of him for over an hour, motioning for the barkeep to bring another.

"Here, this one is for you," Frank said, pushing the other glass toward him. "I ordered two, one for you and one for me. This is all I want." Frank looked away and continued. "Okay, whatever. Sherry. We watched the movie, some of it, anyway. Then she told me she couldn't go against her daddy; she didn't want to sneak around behind his back. So, we're going to wait."

"Wait? I thought you said you weren't going to see her again?" Charles frowned.

"Yeah, we'll write. She said she would write me, anyway. If she does, I'll write her back. We'll do that for a while, at least until she has another birthday. Then we'll see. She told me, Charley, she told me that she thinks she loves me," Frank said but didn't sound happy about it.

"Okay, Frank. That makes me think she's got a good head on her shoulders. She's not fickle, you know? See, Sherry hasn't known you that long. She needs to think about it. That's good, Frank, that's good. Ya'll write and see where it goes." Charles reached over and patted his friend on the back.

"Yeah. Let's just wait and see if Sherry does write me," Frank said, finishing his beer and standing. "I'm heading out, just going to take a walk. See you at the bus, in what," he said, looking down at his watch, "about an hour?"

"Sure. I'm going to write a quick letter home while I'm waiting. Looks like they might draft Mike, my sister's husband, into the Army. He's not too keen on the idea. I don't know; if I grew up where he did, I might feel the same way." Charles shrugged.

"What? Where did he grow up?" Frank stopped on his way out the door.

"His parents were what you call military, I guess. His dad was a teacher at Columbia Military Academy, and his mom worked there, too. Heard of it?" Charles looked over at Frank.

"Nah, but I get it, I guess. You only want so much of someone always telling you what to do," Frank replied, turning back to the hallway.

"I'll see you at the bus," Charles said, holding up his glass. "Thanks for the beer."

Watching Frank walk out the door, he was relieved that his friend seemed to be in better spirits. Not exactly happy, but hopeful.

Jan. 9, 1944
Sunday

Dear Mother, Dad, Sarah & Joe,

Well, here I am in town again. I came over to see a movie; that is about all there is to do around here, go to the show and sit around the canteen. Everything is about the same up here. It is still plenty cold, it was 24 degrees below zero the other morning, but it is only about zero degrees today; this is a warm day. I went skating on the river. I just happened to go down there and a kid loaned me his skates and I skated for a while. Mississippi River is about the size of Duck River up here. I go skating on the lake at school and it is about 1 ½ miles wide and they have a tractor and grader out on it scrapping it off. You need not worry about the ice breaking up. Here it is frozen about 4 to 5 feet deep. This weather isn't like it is in Tennessee. They drive cars on the Mississippi River, pulling a sled behind them.

The snow doesn't even melt up here. I think I must be a eskimo because I don't mind this cold weather at all. I don't even wear my long underwear and I never get cold.

I was reading in the paper where they were going to take everybody from 18-22 in the Army. Mike may have to go to the Army. But it won't hurt him at all, in fact it would be good for him.

I had a letter from Dalcomb today. He said he was getting along just fine.

Mother, I am sorry you didn't like my pictures. I thought they were pretty good. Louise said she really liked hers. You can't expect a ugly person like me to make a pretty picture. I guess you could tell I have gained weight. I am still gaining, too. I had to have my pants let out. They got so tight I couldn't hardly button them. I don't look much bigger but I am getting lots harder and that increases my weight a lot.

Tell Sarah to take care of herself and if she has a boy, I will send him a football or something,

Love, Charles

January 19, 1944

Dear Mother, Dad, Sarah & Joe,

Mother, I don't want you to start worrying about me again. I know I am in lots better shape physically and mentally. I like this army alright. If I ever get to be a lieutenant, I think I will just stay in the Army for the next 20 years and then retire with a pension.

It sure is bad about everybody having to go to the Army. I hate to see poor old Avery Green have to go to the Army.

He sure don't want to go. The only thing I hate about this Army is that I didn't get married before I got in here. I think I will get married just as soon as I get where I can.

Love, Charles

Frank handed the letter back to Charles. "You don't think you should say something else? Maybe you and Louise have already talked about it?"

"What else is there to say? I'm going to tell her all about it. Sometime. Heck, I don't know why I'm so worried. She likes Louise, and Louise likes her." Charles shook his head.

"It's because it's your mom. You're her little boy," Frank said, grinning.

Charles nodded. "I know. It doesn't matter how old we are, I guess. She worries all the time about everything. This war has her scared to death of losing us. I keep telling her not to worry, but she doesn't listen. I figure me getting married is just something else for her to worry about."

"Maybe you're looking at this wrong. If you and your girl were married, you would have someone to take care of you, right? Maybe your mom will be glad about that. My mom wouldn't care one way or the other; I'm pretty sure. Married or not married, she's rid of me, I reckon," Frank said, seeming not to care.

Charles looked over at his roommate. There wasn't an answer to that. Frank didn't want one; he was just stating a fact and had reconciled to it. Maybe that was better.

Charles couldn't comprehend families that weren't close like his. How could you not care about these people? People that were your blood?

"What about this classification stuff? Are you worried?" Frank asked.

Orders were given out sporadically; without warning, the recruits would receive new instructions. Charles knew how Frank felt.

"Sure, I'm worried. They have all the pilots they need, and they'll be tough on us. We've got three more weeks of classes, and then we start flying." Charles pointed up to the ceiling.

"Right, two weeks of non-stop flying and studying. What, probably March, the first of March? I hope it's a little bit warmer around here then." Frank shrugged. "You into flying that little Cub?"

"You bet. I can hardly wait. And then I want to fly one of those big 4-motor bombers." Charles sat back and stared at Frank. "Did you ever think we would be doing this? When you were a kid, I mean. This war. I try not to think about it, but it's always there. I think about flying. I want to fly. And I want to defend my country. But I didn't think about this when I was a little kid wanting to fly planes."

"Nope, me neither. I don't want to. We do what we're told, Charley. We go where they tell us and do what they tell us. It's that simple." Frank stood and walked over to the door.

"Where are you going?" Charles asked. It was late; time to sleep what little they could before the wake-up call.

"Just to the pit," Frank said, pulling the door closed.

Frank had just returned from the latrine a few minutes ago. Either he was sick or didn't want to continue the conversation. Frank wasn't much for sharing how he felt; when he did offer something personal, Charles tried to be patient and quiet, letting him get it out. War buddies. A different kind of friendship, he supposed. And it would get even more intense, he thought, when you were overseas.

Some things were hard to think about. War was hard to think about. But it invaded almost every moment in some way.

8

Minnesota

Jan.25, 1944
Tuesday night

Dear Mother, Dad, Sarah & Joe,

I received your letter the other day and was glad to hear from you. I had a letter from Dalcomb the other day but he didn't say anything about his stomach. He said he would finish school about the first of March, so I guess he and I will finish about the same time.

If I get through classification I guess when I come home I will be flying a big 4 motor bomber (I hope). I am still doing pretty good in my studies. I wish the rest wasn't any harder than this. I could get by just fine. I haven't gained any weight in about 3 weeks. I guess I am as big as I am going to get. They sure have been giving us heck in PT. I am hard as I ever was in my life and these calisthenics still nearly kill me. Boy, this cadet training is no good for weak people.

How is Sarah feeling? Tell Joe he should score more than 3 points. Tell him to shoot more. Guess I had better study a little now. Good night.

Love, Charles

January 28, 1944
Friday

Dear Mother, Sarah, Dad and Joe,

Well, I guess I am a Uncle Charles now. I received your telegram this morning. I sure am glad Sarah had a boy and that they both are doing fine. I just knew she was going to have a boy all the time. Thanks a lot for the telegram, I sure was glad to get it. I will send him something when I go to town this weekend. Tell Sarah I said congratulations,

Love, Charles

January 30, 1944
Sunday

Dear Mother, Dad, Sarah, Baby, and Joe,

How is my little nephew getting along? I came to town last night and tried to find something for the baby but I didn't get to town until at 8:30 pm and most all the stores were closed. I came to town early this morning and went to church. This is the first time since I have been here that I have gone to church. I hate to have to come to town so early and have to stay all day. There isn't anything to do in this town at all on Sunday. I think I will go to the movies this afternoon.

I read a little of the war news and I believe that this old war will be over in a few months now. They told us at school Saturday that they had about all the pilots they need now and that they were washing out about 75% of the men now. That didn't sound very encouraging. I sure hope I can get through this training. But I may get washed out for something. If I am washed out I want to be a aviation mechanic.

I am still doing pretty good in my studies. I am next to the highest average in my class. I didn't ever think I could make very good grades but if you study you can get by easy. I sure wish I had studied harder in high school. Tell Joe I said he had better pass everything this year or I will be ready to whip him when I get home.

Mother, it is too bad about Jack Poag. I guess they will send him back across if he has been in the hospital that long. I didn't know he had a nervous breakdown. I don't think it is any use in you ever worrying about me having a nervous breakdown. I don't let anything worry me that much. I guess I am too dumb.

That's about all I know. Guess I had better go to the movie.

Love, Charles

"Who's Jack?" Frank asked, handing the letter back to Charles. Charles wasn't sure why he gave his letters home to Frank to read before he sent them, but he did most of the time. Charles guessed it might make him feel like he was part of a family. The letters to Louise, well, that was different. Frank seemed to get that, too, although he asked Charles' opinion on letters he wrote to Sherry.

"Jack's my cousin. He's been over there, well, about a year, maybe. I'm not sure. I kind of lost track. They live in California." Charles folded the letter and placed it in the envelope. He would post it on the way to the movie theater.

"Your cousin must have seen some bad stuff to have a nervous breakdown," Frank shook his head.

"I think a lot of them have seen some bad stuff. We might see some bad stuff, too, Frank. I try not to think about it," Charles replied.

"Me, too. Still, you got to feel sorry for those guys, like your Jack. Maybe some guys just can't take it, or maybe it's too nasty to be around for very long. I've heard rumors about the Japs, starving people, even turning into cannibals, some of them. Horrible stuff. And the Germans, rounding up people and putting them in prison," Frank said, staring out the canteen window.

"Yeah, there's stuff we don't know. Probably stuff we are glad we don't know. I guess we might find out," Charles said, standing up. "Come on, let's go check out the Hitchcock movie; what is it?" Changing the subject seemed to be best.

"Lifeboat," Frank said. "But I've heard it's about a German guy. I don't know if I care to see anything about a German."

"Oh, come on. We'll see if it's any good. If it's not, we'll leave. It's supposed to have some good people," Charles replied.

"That Tallulah dame is in it. Worth a try, I guess. Nothing else to do around here," Frank said, looking up and down the street, hoping to see Sherry, Charles guessed.

World War II

Names associated with heroic efforts, both wins and losses, were bantered about in training barracks and homes across the United States. Americans were familiar with the exploits, the few of which were reported, of General Eisenhower, General George Patton, and an aviation legend, Major General Jimmy Doolittle. Doolittle was a United States Army Air Corps commander and led the raid on some of the Japanese main islands in April of 1942, just four short months after the attack on Pearl Harbor. The raid proved to the Japanese that their homeland could also be attacked and was heralded as a major morale booster for the armed services.

Doolittle's heroics were discussed in living rooms across the country, and none so much as in the homes of those that had young men training to be pilots or already in the skies above war-torn countries. However, those on military bases had more timely news reports of action overseas. Many bombing runs were launched by the United States aimed at the manufacturing heart of Germany. The raids had to be conducted in daylight for the drops to be accurate. Fighter escorts were rare, and the bombers flew in tight formations allowing each bomber to provide – for one another – defensive machine-gun fire. American bomber crew losses were high, and some missions resulted in a staggering loss of men and equipment. The introduction of the P-51 Mustang plane gave hope to the military leaders; this fighter plane had enough fuel to make a round trip to Germany's heartland and would be instrumental in reducing loss of life and injuries later in the war.

While each young man yearning to fly the skies for their country pushed aside their fear of approaching the enemy, leaders across the military searched for ways to inspire and energize the war effort. Stories of torture of prisoners of war and the high casualty lists had to be overcome with words and stories of heroism. Acts of bravery came not only from those flying the bombers but also from the other military branches. A young naval combat officer fighting the Japanese in the South Pacific was tested when his quick decisions led to saving lives. This young man, John F. Kennedy, denied the hero's standing, saying, "It was involuntary. They sank my boat." Heralded among the soldiers, men were inspired by heroic efforts of others fighting against the evil empires of Germany and Japan.

Minnesota

February 5, 1944

Dear Mother, Sarah, Dad, Joe & baby,

I am getting along just fine, I guess. We will leave here March 11. I also guess we will start flying in about 2 ½ weeks. I guess you have read in the paper where they are going to close down a lot of these colleges. They are going to close this one in June. They have also raised the standard for cadets back to pre-war standards. They said they have all the pilots they need. I know it is going to be really hard to get this course now. I still believe I can make it but it sure is going to be tough.

Dad, thanks a lot for the letter. I really like to hear from you and Joe. I wish you both would write more. I don't hardly have time to write at all. I write Louise every day, and she also writes me. So I get a letter everyday. It sure helps when you can get mail every day.

Love, Charles

February 13, 1944

Dear Mother, Dad, Sarah, Joe and Baby Michael,

How is everything in Columbia? I sure do have a time trying to call you at home. Every time I call I either can't hear you or you can't hear me. I think it is someone on that line from town trying to call the operator and listening on the phone or something. Because I can hear the Columbia operator good when she is talking.

Well, we are the next class to leave here. We leave one month from yesterday. I only have one week and three days more of classes then we start flying. I sure hope me and Dalcomb can get through classification but it sure is going to be tough. They have all the pilots they need and so they are washing out about 50% of the men who go through classification. I guess if I get washed out they will send me to aviation mechanics school.

Joe, what kind of car do you have now. Mother told me that you traded Dalcomb's car. What is yours like now. Are you running around much. Boy, stay out of this Army as long as you possibly can. I think we will have Germany whipped this year. But I believe it will take at least one to two years more to whip Japan. And you may be 18 years old by then.

I sent Louise a box of candy for Valentine. How did you like your candy? It wasn't very good but that is all I could get.

Well, Dad, how is everything getting along? I sure wish I could be back home working. I was doing lots more good at work than I am doing in this Army so far. But I guess maybe from now on I will be helping more. When I learn to fly you and mother better get ready because I am sure going to take you for a nice ride even if I have to tie you both in.

I hope Sarah and the baby gets along alright. I will probably get to come home and see him when he starts walking and talking. I want to hear him say 'Uncle Charley.'

Love, Charles

Charles laid the letter on his desk and walked down the hall to the head. They wouldn't be here that much longer; sharing the head with so many others didn't seem to be such a big deal anymore, especially after living in a tent.

He returned to the room to find Frank sitting on the edge of his bed, reading the letter Charles had folded up. He started to object but held back the words. Frank had only received two letters from Sherry, and it had been more than a week since he had received the last one. Mail was a rarity for Frank, while Charles received something almost daily.

Frank handed the letter back to Charles. "You sound different in that letter," he said, staring at Charles.

"Different? What do you mean?" Charles shook his head. "It's just me, same as always. What's different about it?"

"I don't know; maybe it's just that you sound homesick. Like you want to be back home, working there, not in the Army anymore. I know, I know," Frank said, holding up his hands. "You usually sound like you're okay with being here. Almost excited about being here. Yeah, we might not get to be flyboys. I think they'll catch on that you're kind of down."

Charles looked down at the letter. "Yeah, maybe."

"Hey, not on me. You write what you want, Charley. It's your family," Frank shrugged.

"Thanks for the tip. I must be careful what I say, especially to my mother. She worries all the time," Charles said.

"Yeah, I know. Momma's little boy," Frank said.

February 19, 1944
Saturday night

Dear Mother, Dad, Sarah, Joe and Baby,

It is another clear cold day up here. I have just about had enough of this cold weather. Mother, I don't want you and Dad to worry about me or Dalcomb either. This Army isn't so bad. In fact, it is lots better than I was expecting. I am getting better food and as good a place to live as I was when I was at Vultee working, and I am in better shape physically than I have been in my life.

I wish you would stop that worrying before there is anything to worry about out of the two million men in the Air Corp. There is a lot of them who are over there fighting all the time who are going to come back in better shape than they were when they left and I am going to be one of them. I don't believe anybody gets killed until his time comes and if it is my time I would have gotten killed if I had been home with you.

Mother, don't worry about me going to California. I always wanted to go to California anyway. And I won't be there for about 2 or 3 months then I will probably be sent to Texas. If Louise comes out to California I am going to get married. I don't know whether it is the best thing to do or not but I had just as soon be married in the Army as to be single. She has been saving her money so I think we will be able to get by alright. I want her to stay with me. She can get a job and I think she can make enough to live on. I will probably have to use some of the money I have saved but I think I just as well use it now while I can enjoy it. There is going to be a lot of ways to make money for at least ten years after this war is over.

I think Louise is the sweetest girl I ever met and I believe she will make me a good wife. I guess everybody has to take that chance when they get married. When this war is over I guess I will come home and get a farm and me and Dad can start farming.

I believe Dalcomb will get through alright. I believe I had just as soon be a gunner as anything. Any airplane job is twice as safe as on the ground. So far in this war it has been about one hundred men killed on the ground to every man killed in the air. (I learned that in military class.)

Love, Charles

Love, Charles

After reading the letter, Frank didn't have much to say other than, "It's about time you told her you're getting hitched."

Charles nodded. He had read Frank's letter to Sherry and offered little in response to Frank's questions if the letter needed to say anything else. Sherry had finally written him a long letter, professing how much she cared for him and that she had decided to wait for him to return to Minnesota after he finished. Although this was not exactly what Frank wanted to hear, he accepted that she at least cared about him.

"Think she'll really wait?" He asked Charles.

"Well, let's see. Do you think you will wait? What about when you see one of these California girls? You might feel different, too," Charles answered.

"Nope. It's Sherry. I knew it the first minute I saw her," Frank replied.

Charles shook his head. "Just don't say the big word until she does."

"What's that? Gettin' married? I ain't that dumb, Charley boy. I want to marry her, gosh, yes. But I know it's too soon for that. You said it, and you're right. I can't rush it; I'll scare her and her daddy, too." Frank took a deep breath.

"Well, yeah, that too. But I was talking about the love word. You know, have you told her you love her? I didn't see that in her letter; she just keeps talking about how much she cares about you."

"She wouldn't wait for me if she didn't love me, right?" Frank looked at Charles, obviously wanting agreement.

"But she didn't say it, did she?" Charles pushed, observing that Frank had avoided the question. So, he probably had told her he loved her.

Charles had waited as long as he could before he told Louise, and then he couldn't contain himself any longer. The look she had given him, a smile that lit up the world for him, was all he needed. She loved him; she told him she couldn't imagine loving anyone the way she did him.

Comparing his relationship with Louise to Frank and Sherry wasn't fair. Charles knew that and felt sorry that Frank had to deal with not knowing how someone felt. The complete peace of knowing that the woman you care about above all others is absolutely, positively in love with you is something everyone should have. Few probably get it, he realized, especially during war. He had heard the stories. Once you got deployed overseas, the letters back and forth weren't enough for some of the girls. Yank, the Army weekly had an article about 'brush-off clubs' several months ago, and the Times had called them 'Dear John' letters. Charles didn't want Frank to get in too deep and go through that.

9

Minnesota

Pete, a new recruit that had stopped by to talk, hurried out the door to their room, not bothering to respond to Frank's barrage of cursing.

"Come on, Frank, don't be so hard on the kid," Charles cautioned.

"I don't have time for his crazy talk, worry about this, worry about that. Man, I just want to lay here, me and my bucket. No talk, no questions, no asking if I need anything. I don't need nothing, just quiet, please," Frank responded.

"You might need to empty that bucket sometime soon. Pete probably would have done that for you if you had been a little nicer to him," Charles said, but as softly as he could. Frank wasn't only vomiting; he said his head was hurting, too. Most of the cadets were sick after the flying gymnastics, flipping, spinning, and stalls in the air, but that had been yesterday. Frank was still sick; maybe he had a bug.

Thankful he hadn't gotten sick, Charles sat down at his desk. It wasn't a chore to write this letter; sometimes, he felt duty-bound to write even though he was exhausted, but not tonight.

It had been a good day, even though it snowed last night, and he didn't get to fly.

February 26, 1944
Saturday night

Dear Mother, Dad, Sarah, Joe and Baby Michael,

Well, Mother, your son is a old flying ace now. I have 4 ½ hours of flying in. I went to the airport Tuesday and flew 1 ½ hours. Then I went back Wednesday but the wind was so hard we couldn't fly. So Thursday I got in 2 hours more, then yesterday I got one more hour. Boy, I really like to fly. I have had stalls, spins, s turns, and everything yesterday. I landed and took off about 6 times. The first thing Monday morning I have a check flight. I can do pretty good flying that little old cub. Nearly all the fellows got sick. My roommate really got sick, he upped all day. It don't make me sick at all. I guess I haven't got enough sense to get sick, I really like it.

It snowed here last night and the snow is about 8 inches deep now. We were suppose to fly today but the weather was too bad.

I guess I will leave here March the 15th, I sure will be glad when I get through this classification. It sure is going to be tough. I guess Louise will come out to see me about May 19th. I sure will be glad to see her; I wish you could come out too but that sure is a long way. If I get sent to Texas, I will be lots closer to home any way. Maybe you and dad can come out then. When I finish this training I will get about 2 months furlough. I believe the war will be almost over by that time.

Mother, how much money do I have left now? If I get married I guess I will have to use some of it until we can get *settled down. I think we can get along alright after we get married. If I finish this training I will start making about $340 per month and I know I can live on that, also save money.*

I did pretty good in my classes here. I have above a 90 average in almost everything. I am going to write Joe before long. He better get to work in school. If he even thinks about quitting school he is crazy. He would not be able to get a job anywhere after this war without a high school education. That laying out of school doesn't sound very good. I think he is getting a little too big for his age. He is still a boy. He never could get in the Air Corps without a high school education. I can't see why he can't make good grades.

Mother, don't worry about me getting married. I think I am old enough and I think Louise is the sweetest girl I know. We can get by alright I know.

Love, Charles

Tricia Cundiff

World War II

News from across the oceans continued to concern Americans at home. With each victory came another defeat, and the rebounds of emotion were exhausting even in the most patriotic of families. While ground and naval forces continued to advance slowly, attentions were on the air as the Combined Chiefs of Staff granted General Eisenhower control over the Allied Air Forces in Europe. Eisenhower, along with his designated Air Chief Marshall Arthur Tedder, was the main topic of conversation around families' dinner tables in the United States and abroad. Winston Churchill, the revered Prime Minister of the UK, voiced some objection to the appointments of Eisenhower and Tedder, but the control was affirmed. By April 1944, Allied airmen were achieving air superiority over Europe.

With more dependable communication systems, Americans could obtain the most recent news reports with radio stations broadcasting the victories and concerns from the war front. Little changed, however, from World War I in how soldiers communicated with their families. Handwritten letters, some many pages long, would sometimes take weeks to arrive back home, and letters sent to soldiers even longer because of the movement of the units.

While victories were celebrated and assurances of an end to the madness of war abounded, mothers and fathers across the nation mourned the loss of sons. Families dreaded the knock at the door and the sorrowful man holding the telegram.

Love, Charles

March 5, 1944
Sunday

Dear Mother, Dad, Sarah, Joe and baby,

I finished up my flying this week, I had my final 10 hours check ride Friday. I guess I did alright because I was recommended for pilot training by my instructor. I took some pictures out at the airport while I was flying. How do you like those flying suits we had? They are all leather and sheepskin lined. You wear your regular uniform under the suit so you stay nice and warm. It sure was cold up here while we were flying; it was below zero most of the time. I sure did like that flying. I hope I get through classification. They say it is hard to get through now.

My final average in math was 92, Geography 94, physics 93, and English 88. Public speaking 89 and I was in excellent class in my last physical training score. This Army has helped me a lot both mentally and physically.

In my check flight Friday, I took off and landed, did rectangular course, five turns, spins (they sure are fun, I had to spin 4 ½ turns), also power on stalls and power off stalls. I flew a 'cub' the first five hours and then I flew a Army 'grasshopper' the last five hours. We had to wear that parachute all the time. But nobody has had to use one out at this airport.

Tell Joe to learn how to use that slide rule I sent home. You can work almost any math on it.

Love, Charles

March 5, 1944
Sunday night

Dear Mother,

I wrote you while I was in town and I didn't realize until after I had got back to school tonight that this is the day 54 years ago one of the sweetest persons in the world was born. Happy Birthday mother, you are the sweetest mother in this world.

Love, Charles

Frank shrugged when Charles offered him the letter to read. Sealing both letters and putting them on the desk to post the next day, Charles laid back on his bunk. "You ran that kid off," he said.

"Not fair. Just stated facts. I can't help if he can't take it," Frank responded.

"I don't think he liked being called 'Little Bo Pete,'" Charles answered but held back a laugh.

"That's on him." Frank stood and stretched. "He was ready to bug out the night I was sick as a dog. Bug out of the whole thing. Couldn't you tell? I don't know how he made it this far."

The recruit had been placed in their room and had lasted only one day. "I'm glad they had another room for him to go to. Some guys got private rooms around here, and they like it," Charles said.

"Saying you want a private room? I can move, you know. There are empty beds down the hall; we've lost a few. You know that old guy on the end? He's gone back home. Discharged right out of here. Something bad must be wrong with him," Frank shook his head.

"Nah, I reckon you can stay. But I have to tell you; I think Louise will make a much better roommate." Charles grinned.

Love, Charles

"Yeah, I just bet she will. So, when is it going to happen? The big day? How's your mommy taking her little boy getting hitched?" Frank threw a pillow at Charles.

"She's coming around," Charles answered. "And you'll be the first to know when the big day is. What about Sherry?" Charles asked, changing the direction of the conversation. "Did you write her back?"

"Yeah. It's all good. Her daddy hasn't changed his mind, and you know, I get it. Why would he want his daughter mixed up with some goofball that might not come back from the war?"

Charles was surprised at Frank's question. Thankful that Frank was trying to see the father's point of view for his daughter, he could see that Frank, too, was growing up in the man's Army. You had no choice, he thought.

"You're right," Charles answered, throwing the pillow back at Frank's head, "especially a goofball like you."

"She says she's going to wait for me. I believe her, I think. Dammit, I don't want to think about that right now. Up for some cards? A few quick hands. The guys down the hall have a game going."

"Nah, I'm done," Charles answered. "I've had a full day. One short letter to Louise and I'm asleep. Go on; have a good time. Just don't lose all your money!"

"Not a chance. Okay, write your kissy, kissy letter. Tell her she's missing out on the real man down here – send her my picture, huh?" Frank laughed as he left the room.

Charles laid back in his bunk. He had already written his letter to Louise; he just needed to finish it. He wished he could just talk to her for more than a few minutes at a time. Soon, he thought.

Tricia Cundiff

March 9, 1944
Thursday night

Dear Mother, Dad, Sarah, Joe & baby –

Dalcomb wrote me yesterday and he said he had six hours of flying in and liked it fine. I sure did like it, and hope I get classified as a pilot.

I guess Sarah has gone home by now. When you write me again, send me her new address. I hate about Sarah's baby being sick. I guess all babies are sick most of the time while they are small. I bet you will sure miss Sarah. I would like to have been home and seen the baby before she went home.

Mother, I hope you don't mind me getting married. It may not be the best thing to do. But I have decided it can't be too bad. I think Louise is about the nicest girl I ever met. I believe she will make me a good wife.

Tell Sarah not to be in any hurry about that money she borrowed because I am not going to use much of my money, if I can help it. I believe we can almost get by on what I made if I don't get washed out.

I am sending you a group picture of my flight. I bet you can't even find me. I am getting big and ugly.

Love, Charles

10

California

"I'm sick of buses. I would be just fine if I never have to ride another one," Frank said as he picked up his duffel. "The seats were harder than the last bus we rode. I feel like I could sleep a week straight."

"You got it," Charles agreed. "Come on. Let's go find out which barracks we've got. No more rooms like we had in St. John's. This is the real deal. The real Army. We're here, Frank. I hope we make it."

> *March 15, 1944*
> *Wednesday*
>
> *Dear Mother, Dad & Joe,*
>
> *Well, I finally got out here. It sure was a long trip. 'But I really enjoyed the whole trip. I saw a lot of pretty country. I wish I could have made the trip by car. The sun is really hot, and it seems like summertime. We got here last night and we had to drill almost all day. My face is really sunburnt again. They are really strict on you here, everything has to be just right. They also washed out about*

half of the people that go through. I sure hope I make it. But I don't know, it sure is going to be hard.

We left St. John's Saturday morning and stopped in Kansas City, Kansas for about 3 hours. Also, we came through Colorado, New Mexico, Arizona and California. Everything is really green around here. You can see the mountains from camp and they are all covered with snow.

We are living in barracks but they are nothing like St. John's. Don't worry about me, mother, I like it out here just fine. This is about the prettiest country I ever saw. And this is a good camp. It is a heck of a lot better than Keesler field. I will write you again just as soon as I get a chance.

Love, Charles

World War II

Two years before Charles Poag arrived in California, the United States Army Air Corps activated Santa Ana Army Air Base and established the training center. The year before Charles arrived, the base was redesignated as the Western Flying Training Command. Santa Ana Army Air Base was an air base without planes, hangars, or runways but was a big component of the basic training camps, being very large. The main objective was to receive air cadets from civilian life and provide basic ground training before moving them to primary aviation schools for flight training.

During the first year of the camp's designation, the SAAAB (Santa Ana Army Air Base) became an Overseas Replacement Depot, hosting Army Air Forces personnel awaiting transport overseas. In late 1943, the Women's Air Service Pilots (WASP) began training along with the Women's Army Corps (WAC) members.

Charles Poag was one of the last cadets to attend SAAAB, as the Pilot School closed in May of 1944, receiving 73,923 cadets since its initial class and graduating 70,464 for flying schools.

California

"Thanks for going to church with me," Charles told Frank, bending down to remove his dress shoes. Surprised that his buddy had said he wanted to go, Charles was glad he did. Frank going with him would be motivating; having the responsibility for someone else would help him stay the course.

"Yeah, it's all right. You know, you have to think God is really on our side, right? Like, if he were down here right now, like Jesus, he would be fighting for our side?" Frank glanced up at Charles and pushed his footlocker close to the foot of his bunk.

Charles was startled. Staring at the blonde flat-top haircut of his friend, he didn't know how to answer. He had wondered himself how God fit into all of this. There was so much hate going around for Germans and Japanese that he wondered how the enemy fared in God's sight.

"I don't know, Frank. I guess Jesus wouldn't want us to be fighting," he answered, shrugging, keeping his voice low. The barracks were filling up with other men. With each barrack holding eighteen when full, there was little privacy.

"Sure, he would. They fought the bad guys in the Bible all the time. You know, like today, what that preacher was saying. Moses and all those people were going to get it, for sure. But then God split apart that lake and boom, they all ran across. Then God drowned all those Egyptians. They should have believed in God, and then they wouldn't have drowned. But nope, they did what their big old Pharaoh told them to do and what did they get for it? Dead, that's what. God was fighting on Moses' side then. Why wouldn't He be fighting on our side now?" Frank was almost whispering, not inviting others in on the conversation.

"I get it. But I don't think it means that God hated all those people. Those people chose to follow other gods or Pharaoh, someone other than Him. So, I guess that's the consequence of not doing the right thing. I think we're doing the right thing. I think God wants us to be in this war. I'm just not sure that God has the same reasons that we do." Charles didn't know how to explain it any better because he wasn't sure he understood it himself. Church had always told him to love one another. That's a hard thing to do in war.

Frank stared at Charles, then nodded. "I guess it does need some more thinking about. But it's not going to stop me from letting those bombs drop out of my P-51 Mustang!"

"You'll do it – if you ever get the chance to fly one of those – because someone told you to do it." Charles didn't say the words but wondered if Frank heard the intention. Just like Pharaoh told the Egyptians to follow the Israelites into the Red Sea. Charles didn't want to think about it. No one did, he supposed. He had no illusions about war and how people died in war. But where was God? A question asked by a lot of people right now, he thought. Never doubting his country's obligation to the Allies and saving people from the evil wants of Germany's Hitler and Japan's Hirohito, Charles often wondered why God couldn't just make those people see their sins and save so many lives.

"I'm beat. You had it better than me, man. At least you were inside yesterday. KP is better than drilling in this heat, I promise you. There's no telling what they have in store for us tomorrow. After all these tests and the blasted gas chamber, I won't be surprised if they throw us out of planes with no chutes," Frank said, loudly enough for the rest of the guys in the barracks to turn around and grin at him.

"KP is not the answer to sweating in the sun, I promise you. Eight in the morning to eight at night, nothing by KP. Yeah, fun, fun, fun. I'm done for, too. Lights out in what? Little less than an hour." Charles grabbed his tablet. He could write a letter in half that time, then hit the head and the shower after it wasn't so crowded.

March 26, 1944
Sunday

Dear Mother, Dad & Joe,

Here it is Sunday again. We are just laying around taking it kindly easy. I had KP all day Saturday. KP isn't as hard here as it was in Basic Training but it is just such long hours. I went to church today, I guess I can go to church more regular around here than I did at St. John's. They have plenty of protestant chapels on the post so I guess I can go almost every Sunday.

Mother, we finished classification Thursday but it will be next Saturday before we find out if we pass or not. I hope I make it, but it sure is going to be tough. They give you all kinds of tests. They sure find out if you are at all nervous or if there is anything else wrong with you. I think I passed my physical alright, my eyes were way above average. I guess our family really have good eyes. We also had a lot of written tests to see how much you know. We had all kinds of coordination tests. I don't think I have any coordination in my left arm because it has been broken, I guess. I don't know if they will wash me out on that or not.

We had to go through the gas chamber again Friday. I sure dreaded that poisonous gas but when you have on your gas mask you can't even tell you are in gas at all. This is just about like basic training all over again. But I don't mind it so bad any more. I guess it is because I am in lots better shape physically than I was when I first came in the Army. This place is lots more strict than St. John's. We are going to be quarantined for about 42 days before we can get off the post.

Mother, I guess Louise will be out here about the last of May or the first of June. I think she can get a job real easy because the papers are just full of ads for secretaries. I will be glad to have her with me. I wish I could have my whole family out here. But it sure is a long way from Tennessee. I may be sent lots closer home after I leave here. Don't worry about me because this is alright out here if it just don't get any worse than this. I think I will stay in the army after the war is over.

Tell Joe to be careful and that he had better pass those studies. I guess I do more studying in a week than he does in 3 months and have to do a hundred other things besides.

Be good and don't worry about me. I can get along alright. I have for 22 years anyway!

Love, Charles

Frank was still awake when Charles returned from the shower. Soft murmurings could be heard throughout the barracks, as well as some snoring. "I got a letter from Sherry," Frank said as Charles crawled into the small cot beside his.

"Yeah? What did she say?" Charles asked.

"She said she wants to come to California and be with me. She said she would let me know when she was coming," Frank said hesitantly.

"Really? Wow," was all that Charles could manage.

"I'm not sure it's a good idea," Frank said slowly.

"Yeah, me, either. Is her father okay with it?" Charles was treading lightly.

"I don't think he knows. She's talking about coming here and getting married, getting a job. Then just going wherever I get stationed, I guess." Frank didn't sound very enthusiastic about the prospect.

"Okay, so what do you think about her plan? You said before you wanted her to come with you to California. Of course, you couldn't see her if she were here. We're in quarantine!" Charles reminded his friend.

"I've had time to think about it, and I'm pretty sure it's not a good idea. I just don't know how to tell her. I love her, Charley; I do love her. But what if I go over there and don't come back? Here she is, she's made her father mad, left her mother, and she's all alone. Nobody to take care of her. My mom, well, she hasn't written me since way before we left Minnesota. I haven't even sent her my new address, not that she cares. And if Sherry and I got married, she could have a baby, and I'd be a daddy, and then I might die, and," Frank stopped and took a deep breath.

Charles didn't know what to say. The words, the feelings, they were familiar. It wouldn't be good to tell Frank that every man in love with someone thought about the same things, concerned about not returning from the war zone. Every soldier thought about the ones left behind. And what would happen if they didn't return to them?

Frank waited for a response from Charles and pressed when he didn't get one. "Don't you think about it?"

"Every day," Charles replied.

"And?" Frank asked.

"I guess everybody is different. For me, I just decided that I was not going to let this war put my life on hold. Louise and I, we've talked about it. It's not the same with you and Sherry; I get it. Louise has lots of family support. But Sherry would, too, if something happened to you, Frank. Her parents love her. I guess you just need to talk to her. Call her the first chance you get. I'll pay for the call if you're running short. Tell her everything; tell her how you feel. She has to be a part of the decision you make. She's seventeen now, right? I suppose that's old enough." Charles felt sorry for Frank but had little to offer regarding answers.

"I'm not sure seventeen is old enough, not for Sherry, anyway. She has a lot of growing up to do," Frank replied, turning over in his cot with his back to Charles. His muffled voice returned, "I'll try to call her tomorrow."

You both have a lot of growing up to do, Charles thought. The lights went out in the hallway, and his eyes closed to the room he would call home for the next few weeks.

April 4, 1944
Tuesday afternoon

Dear Mother, Dad, & Joe,

Mother, don't worry about me leaving some money in the bank. I intended to leave at least $200 there for you to use if you need it. If I have to have any more I will turn in a few war bonds. However, I don't think I am going to need any of the money hardly at all. When I get married I will draw about $100 per month. And Louise has saved a little money. She thinks we should use what she has first. I don't believe we will have to use hardly any of our money. I believe Louise can get a job and with the $100 I make per month we can get by just fine.

We are still just laying around drilling and waiting to be classified. They washed out all the pre-service men here yesterday. However they let all the fellows who were in the Air Corps before they got into cadets stay. So I believe Dalcomb will get to finish this course. I sure hope so anyway. They washed out the men who were in the infantry, etc. even if they had passed classification. They all have to go back to their old branch of service. I met a sailor who was in the hospital with Jack Poag. He was also with him over across. His name was Parsons. He came down here to see his boy who was in cadets, but he has already washed out now.

I got a letter from Sarah and she said Mike had to go take his physical exam. I hope Mike don't have to go to the Army but I guess you would be glad to have Sarah back home with you.

Well, write when you can. I wish you were out here in this pretty sunshine. This sure is beautiful weather.

Love, Charles

11

California

April 7, 1944

Dear Mother, Dad, & Joe,

Well, I was classified today and I was classified as a pilot. I sure am glad I got through this classification. It sure was hard, but at least I know I am in good shape physically and mentally.

I don't believe that Dalcomb will be washed out because they are taking all the fellows who were in the Air Corps before they got into cadets. Also the people like myself who came in out of civilian life. I don't think Dalcomb has anything to worry about for a while anyway. I believe he will get to go to classification all right. I sure hope he makes it, but gunner isn't bad at all. I would kindly like to be gunner myself.

I have to go. I will try and write again this week. I sure am glad I made pilot, I sure want to fly. I won't get to fly any until after I leave here though.

Love, Charles

World War II

The world remained glued to news reports of advancements, victories, and defeats, none more so than the men training to join the fight. The strategic wins for the Allies, whether they came from the Army, the Marines, the Navy, or the Air Force, were cause for celebration in barracks across the United States and in homes from coast to coast.

After the Navy had effectively changed the tide of the Pacific War in the Battle of Midway, the reports showed the Allies' progress across the islands. The American public, and families of Allied forces across the world, knew of our men's advancement into the South Pacific islands. The cadets training to join the fight received information about the island-hopping of the Allied Forces, both unreliable rumors and accurate reports.

Airmen flew much more often in the southwest Pacific than in Europe, with a few hours, and sometimes a couple of days, of rest time in Australia. Airfields were a must for the Navy and Air Corps. With the aid of the Army Corps of Engineers, AAF Commander General Hap Arnold created airfields scattered across the southwest Pacific, complete with runways, hangars, radar stations, power generators, barracks, and more. These airfields had to be constructed on tiny coral islands, dense jungles, mud flats, and featureless deserts, sometimes under heavy artillery fire. News of the flights of the pilots and the harsh conditions traveled back to the cadets training to join them in the air, and the fervor heightened to begin their service, saddled by the fear of the unknown ahead. Pushing the uncertainty aside, trainees reveled in the victorious exploits of their forerunners in the air.

Love, Charles

April 11, 1944
Tuesday

Dear Mother, Dad & Joe,

I sure am glad I got through this classification. I never saw so many tests and things we had to go through. We have to go through a pressure chamber in a few days. They pump the air out until it is the same as if you were up 38,000 feet high in a airplane, so they can tell if you are suited for high altitude flying. After you get that high you have to wear oxygen masks. There isn't enough oxygen in the air that high for a person to live unless they wear the masks.

I sure am glad I was classified as a pilot. I sure want to fly if I possibly can. I will have pre-flight school here, it takes 10 weeks and it will probably be about 2 or 3 weeks before I can get in pre-flight. I won't get a chance to fly any more until I leave here and get in primary school. Then I will be in primary 10 weeks, basic 10 weeks and advance 10 weeks. I will get to fly about 60 hours in each of these schools. I may be sent somewhere pretty close to home in one of the schools. I sure hope so anyway.

I sure will be glad when Louise comes out. I wish I could see my whole family but I guess it will be about another 6 months before I will be able to get a furlough. When I start to pre-flight and get married, I will draw $103 per month, counting what I get and what Louise will get so I believe we can almost live on that. It will only cost what it takes for Louise to live on because Uncle Sam buys my clothes, feeds me, and furnishes me a place to sleep.

I had to have about 5 teeth fixed. Boy, your teeth have to be perfect in this Air Corps (everything else too).

Love, Charles

Charles held the phone to his ear, closing his eyes. There was no one in line for the lone phone in the small room; he was alone and had placed the call collect. Louise had insisted in her last letter. A phone call, hopefully uninterrupted, for a long talk. The best they could do for now.

"I agree. Four years is enough. Chaz?" Just hearing her voice was enough for now. He shook his head, laughing.

"Yeah, sweetheart. I'm sorry. It's just so good to hear your voice. It won't be long now. We've waited a long time to be together, and I'm glad you don't want to wait until this crazy war is over," Charles replied.

"When did you know? Really? That you might want to marry me?"

Charles laughed. "Well, let's see," Charles continued, "probably when you asked me!"

"When I asked you? Charles Poag! I didn't ask you!" Louise giggled.

Charles loved the sound of her laugh. "Yeah, yeah, I know. I was so nervous. Let's see. When did I know? Probably when Avery walked in behind you. You couldn't see, but he pointed at you behind your back. You know, the bet. The hundred bucks I still owe him."

"Oh, come on. You didn't even know me then. When did you think you might love me?" Her voice was low and serious.

"That night. I knew I was done for. You were the most beautiful thing I had ever seen. I knew I would try to get you to love me right then. So how long did it take you?"

"Not long. I guess I was a little nervous. I mean, Avery built you up, but I suspected what he was telling me was too good to be true." Her tone was mischievous.

"So, what did Avery tell you?" Charles was curious.

"Well, he said you were tall," Louise said.

"I am kind of tall," Charles replied.

"Yes, you are," Louise said.

"What else?"

"He was right. He said you were a good guy and pretty smart, too."

"Okay, well, that's nice to hear. Did you agree with him?" Charles asked.

"I didn't know you then. I had to find out. You are pretty smart, I guess. You are a good guy. But," Louise stopped.

"But? But what?" He was curious. There were no buts about his feelings for Louise.

"You don't really look like Henry Fonda," Louise said, struggling not to laugh.

"Henry Fonda? Avery said that? That's what you were looking for, huh?" Charles chuckled.

"Of course, but I finally decided you would do," Louise said matter-of-factly.

"Well, thank you. I'm sorry I couldn't meet your expectations, but this dumb face of mine will have to do," Charles countered.

Louise's tone turned serious. "I talked to you for five minutes. Your handsome face put everyone else to shame, including Henry Fonda; bless his heart. It was your heart that made me love you, Chaz. The outside is wonderful. The inside is magnificent. I love you."

"I wish I could talk like you do," Charles said, his heart bursting. "I love you so much; I want to be together forever, you know. When did you know you would marry me? I think you knew before I even asked."

"I did. I knew I would marry you when you took me home to meet your mother and dad. It was clear that it was important to you that your mother and I connect. And we will, I promise. It's hard for her to give up her boys, you know. Even harder than a daughter, I suspect. You're a lot like your mother, I think. Family first. That's when I knew I would spend the rest of my life with you," Louise answered.

"And I want to spend the rest of my life with you. But Louise, you have to know, this war," Charles stopped, taking a deep breath. "I worry. I worry about you mostly if we get married. And I want to get married so very much. But what if, you know, what if," Charles hesitated.

"No, don't say it. You'll come back. If this war is still going on, you'll come back. I won't have it any other way," Louise said, her voice coming across the line with force.

"I have to know that you will be okay. I know you have family, and you'll have my family, too. I can do what I need to if I know you are okay," Charles said softly.

"I will be, I promise. Okay, Chaz, listen to me. Of course, I've thought about it. What woman in these horrible times hasn't? But you know, something could happen to me, too. We could get bombed right here. We don't know where this war is headed. Some days it looks good; others, it looks bad."

"We're not going to let that happen. The war won't come here." Charles interrupted, although he could hear her breath coming in short bursts across the many miles that separated them.

"Don't deny it, Chaz. It could happen. The war is happening all over the world, it seems. But not here, not yet. We don't know if it will or not. But my Chaz, know this. We have the rest of our lives, no matter how long that is. Yes, let's get married. Soon. I love you; I want to be your wife."

Charles remembered all of their long conversation, broken up only when the Sargeant came in and insisted he hang up. They had discussed where Louise would live; he said he would find her a place just as soon as possible. She would drive to California at the end of May or the first of June. Her younger brother, Jack, said he was coming with her so she wouldn't be driving alone. His Louise would be here with him. They would get married. It seemed too good to be true. Finally, now his purpose was clear. A place for Louise to live.

Love, Charles

Charles' reverie was interrupted by Frank bounding in from the shower, throwing his dirty clothes in the hamper.

Frank dropped onto his unmade cot. "I'm not sure I'm glad I let you help me pass physics. Do I really want to do this?"

Charles didn't answer. Although looking forward to many things, he was physically exhausted. It was unusual for him and Frank to have the same duty, especially for 24 hours. Both had guard duty last night and had been functioning on less than an hour of sleep since the previous morning. Since both had passed classification and were now aviation cadets, they passed the day moving into the pre-flight school.

Frank, unfortunately, continued to talk. "I don't know how you're still moving around," he said as Charles sat down on his bunk and bent down to remove his boots. "My feet ache, but I'm too tired to take the boots off. You know we have to be up in just a few hours, right? Five o'clock. At least breakfast is decent. We'll need it for all five of those blasted classes. Then more drilling and PT. Where are you on the parade line?"

Charles looked over at Frank and shrugged, too tired to respond. He just lined up where they told him to in the parade line, marching with his unit. The parade was mandatory every day. Charles didn't know if it was specific to the Santa Ana base or if trainees were in parades across the country every day.

Finally prone on his cot, Charles stared at the ceiling. He was too tired to write Louise or his mom; it would have to wait. Almost as if Frank was reading his mind, he began talking again.

"Coding class is tough, maybe too tough for me. Eight words a minute in code? I'll be lucky to do two. Dot, dot, dash, dash, dot, dot, dot. They all sound the same. And all those airplane identifications? They're all starting to run together. It should be simple; shoot the bad guys. No, no. We need to know what kind of plane is up there, them and us." Frank let out a long sigh.

Charles agreed. The classes were tough, and despite his determination to succeed, he was concerned about coding. But it wouldn't help any to voice that to Frank. "Yeah, it's tough. But we'll get it; keep working at it. My brother says it's not so bad. He's had coding already, so when he gets around to taking it after classification, it will be easy for him." Charles hoped that would be the end of the conversation. He wanted to get what little sleep he could.

"Dalcomb, right? Your brother? Didn't you say he was in Texas now?" Frank must be wired or worried about something; he was usually asleep before Charles.

Charles sighed and sat up on the side of his cot, pulling his paper and pencil from under his bunk. He might as well write a short letter to his mom; Frank would eventually fall asleep.

"Yes, he's in Texas. Still hasn't got through classification. He hopes that'll be done soon," Charles replied and was encouraged when Frank turned over to face the wall after he saw Charles pull out the pencil and paper.

April 24, 1944
Monday

Dear Mother, Dad and Joe,

Well, another hard day. They are really keeping us busy now since I got in pre-flight.

I got out of camp this weekend so I went up to Los Angeles and also I went to a Hollywood canteen. I saw several movie actors. But the city is too big for me. I never saw so many people. That Los Angeles is really a big town. I also looked over Santa Ana, it is a nice little town.

I guess Louise will be starting out about May 28th. I guess she will get here about June the first. I know I will enjoy this Army life a lots better after I am married. I just hope Louise

Love, Charles

don't get lonesome and homesick on me. If she gets a job and works I guess that will help her from being lonesome.

Mother, I want you to send me a few blank checks and also tell me how much I have in the bank. I forgot how much I put in. I don't know how much money I will use but I will leave you at least $200 in the bank. If I need more than I have in cash before I finish this training I will cash in some defense bonds. I want to cash them in before the war is over anyway. I am kindly afraid to keep them after the war. It may be a lot of trouble getting money for them unless you keep them ten years.

I sure am glad Mike is going to be deferred. I like the Army life pretty good. I wouldn't mind staying in after the war.

Love, Charles

Tricia Cundiff

World War II

Mail call was the highlight of many days for the men in the military. It didn't matter where they were stationed. Soldiers and sailors shipped overseas couldn't make phone calls, and most would write several letters each week. It could take up to four weeks for the letter to cross the ocean and be received in the United States, and the process was the same for letters being sent from home to the men overseas.

Orderlies would sort the mail on the roadside, and carts would be wheeled to the front lines to give it to the soldiers. The timing would change daily with the movement of the units and the outcome of each battle. The hope was that the mail could be handed out during the evening meal.

Trainees and men stationed on bases in the continental United States received mail through the postal service rather than the 'Victory Mail' program for World War II. Mail sent and received through the regular postal service was not subject to the censorship of Victory Mail, wherein words, sentences, and sometimes entire portions of letters were marked through with heavy ink.

California

Mail call was welcome on the Santa Ana base. Most of the men stationed there were without family, although several had their wives nearby.

Charles glanced over at Frank; he hoped that the letter Frank was reading was decent and would leave him in a good mood. Most of the time, letters from Sherry would place Frank in a better frame of mind for a day or two, then he would wait on the next one to arrive and become agitated when Charles received a letter almost every day from Louise. Sherry wasn't Louise; he had to remind Frank. His attention went back to his letter from Louise.

Louise had seen his mother and told him that she thought his mother looked better than she had in a long time. That was good to hear. He worried about his mother's health and how she tried to do things she shouldn't. He had tried to call Louise and his mother earlier in the day, but it was going to be a two or three-hour delay, and he couldn't wait that long for the call to go through. The rumor was that he would be changing squadrons the next day, and he wanted to send them his new address. He would write both when he finished reading his mail but would wait until tomorrow to mail them.

Charles looked over at Frank again. It was incredible that they had been together for as long as they had, but it didn't appear that Frank was moving with him to another squadron. They would still see each other occasionally, but he worried about his roommate. Most of the time, he could convince Frank to be objective and not jump to conclusions.

Charles supposed every recruit needed that reassurance and realized that without the letters he received from his mother and Louise, he would probably be in worse shape than Frank. How letters could be that important was unknown until it was all you had.

Opening the last letter he received, a rare one from Dalcomb, he again glanced over at Frank, who was now staring at the ceiling. Let him think about it and talk when he wants to, Charles thought, turning his attention to the letter from Dalcomb.

"Oh, no," he said out loud without realizing it.

"What is it?" Frank said, turning and sitting up on the bunk.

Charles looked at Frank, shaking his head. "It's Dalcomb. He washed out of classification. I figured he would be a better shot at it than me." He read a few more sentences. "It looks like he's going to do something with radio."

"That's bad, man. Sorry for your brother," Frank said, sounding genuinely concerned.

Charles looked over at his bunkmate. He and Frank had become good friends throughout their training. Shared concerns and problems, celebrated good news, and sometimes talked deep into the night about plans for the future. Charles had shared his faith with Frank and knew that a seed had been planted when Frank began attending church. As abrasive as Frank could be, Charles knew that he was a good man deep inside and wanted only the best for him.

"Yeah, well," Charles said. "Sherry? She doing okay?" He asked because he didn't know what to say about Dalcomb. He could only imagine how bad his brother felt right now.

"She's good, I guess. Planning on coming here this summer. I've tried to tell her not to come, trying to convince her to wait, but she's pushing it, I guess, with her parents. I just hope she really wants to come to see me and not so much to get away from her parents." Frank looked at Charles, wanting a reply from his friend but not sure he wanted to hear it.

"I know how much I want Louise here, and she wants to be here, too. I don't know what to tell you, Frank. You know Sherry a lot better than I do." Charles replied.

"That's just it. You were right from the beginning, Charley. I don't know her that well. It was too fast, and now I'm right in the middle." Frank put his head in his hands.

"Then tell her, Frank. You've got to tell her before it goes too far," Charles urged.

"Tell her what?" Frank looked up at Charles. "Tell her that I thought I loved her? I might love her. I guess I love her. But now, I don't know. I'm not sure. Maybe when I see her again, I'll feel different."

Charles looked at his friend. There was nothing he could do to help. Frank was going to have to figure out this one on his own. Pulling out paper and pencil, he needed to start on his letters to Louise, Dalcomb, and his mother.

"Write her back, Frank. Tell her something, but I think you must try to convince her to stay home until you're both sure what you want."

April 30, 1944
Sunday

Dear Mother, Dad & Joe,

I had a letter from Dalcomb and he told me he washed out in classification. I sure did hate to hear that. I had rather he had made it than me. But I guess it is for the best; he can have a better chance of making a living after the war if he is in radio. They are going to have so many pilots you will never be able to get a job as a pilot. I don't think he will have to go across a bit quicker, and he will stand a better chance of getting back than he would if he was a pilot. Don't worry about him or me either. I know everything will work out for the best.

I sure will be glad when I can get home and see you, Dad and Joe. I guess it will be about 6 more months before I can get home unless I am sent back close to home for training.

Love, Charles

12

California

Early May, and time was running out. Louise would be here in just a few weeks. He had to try and do something soon, or it would be too late.

Frank looked at Charles, shaking his head, reluctance spread across his face. "You want me to help you do what?"

"Well, see, I want to give Louise a wedding ring. I want it to be a nice, wide, gold band. One for both of us. Matching bands, you know? But the guy at the jewelry store didn't have what I wanted. It's a skinny little thin band, and I want a wide one. But he told me if I could bring him some gold, he could melt it down and make me two bands. So I've got to find some gold stuff."

"What makes you think I can get you more gold trinkets than you can get yourself? All the guys like you; I don't know of a single nut in this man's Army that doesn't like you. Now there's a bunch of them that would like a chance to take a swing at me," Frank said indifferently.

Charles laughed. "That's because you go around trying to get a rise out of anybody about anything. They've all got your number, Frank. Okay, okay. I'll see what I can round up." Charles's hopes were high as he headed out the door to find the rest of the boys in his unit.

Two hours later found Frank still on the bunk, staring at an old newspaper one of the other cadets had left. Charles came in and pulled two gold cuff links out of his pocket. "That's it. That's all I could get. Sgt. Booker said to try a dentist's office. They use gold to fix teeth all the time. I bet I have some in my mouth right now, but I suppose I should leave it be; after getting my teeth fixed to suit the Army. Off to a dentist's office. Want to go with me?"

"Nah, I'm bushed. Going to try and call Sherry in a few minutes. Good hunting, buddy!" Frank laid down the newspaper and looked over at Charles. "Gold from a dentist. I've heard lots of crazy stuff before," he said, laughing and shaking his head.

Charles had his list of dentists' offices; only two were close enough to allow him enough time to get there and back. The first one was not open; a sign on the door indicated that the office wouldn't be open until the first of June. Who closes a dentist's office for a month, he wondered. It could be anything; he reminded himself. During this war, anything could have happened to a family member. It was not surprising to find wreaths and flags in the windows of businesses and homes. A flag hung in the dentist's window; someone the dentist knew was serving. Charles said a quick prayer for the family, the soldier, and whatever they were going through now.

The second dentist was only three blocks away. When Charles arrived, the door was open, but the dentist was with a patient. After speaking to the lady at the front desk, he sat in the waiting room and looked at the papers on the side table next to his chair. Newspapers, all recent editions, with words of war across the front page. Charles had read all of them. He noticed a small framed picture of a man in uniform on the lady's desk and a wedding band on her finger. The war is touching every corner of the world, Charles thought to himself.

Love, Charles

Less than half an hour passed before the door to the back of the office opened, and a young woman with a child came out; the little boy with a broad smile as he displayed two front teeth missing.

"Corky! Just look at you! Aren't you the handsome one! I bet you want a new box of crayons, don't you?" The lady reached into a bag behind her desk and handed the little boy a box of crayons. "Here, this is a special box, you know. You hang onto these crayons, Corky. They have a special color in them called Gamboge Yellow. My sister works in Pennsylvania, where they make these, and that color is gone now! They aren't making that color any longer because they can't get the right stuff for it." The woman looked up at the boy's mother. "Just like everything else, I guess. More stuff that we can't get anymore."

Charles watched the boy open the box of crayons and study the colors. He couldn't imagine that all of the sticks wouldn't be used up within a month. The receptionist ushered the mother and the boy out the door and nodded at Charles. He followed her into a small office adjacent to the patient room. Dr. Briggins stood behind a small desk and offered his hand to Charles, which seemed to be at least a good sign that the dentist would listen to his request.

Dr. Briggins listened while Charles explained his reason for being there and smiled when Charles' story ended with a request to purchase any gold that Dr. Briggins might have.

"I would love to help you out, son, if I could. But I can't part with any of the gold I have right now; it's in short supply as it is. I'm turning people away who don't need immediate dental work done because of material; I can't sell any to anyone. Other dentists have contacted me for any gold I might have, and I don't have any extra. I'm so sorry," he said.

Charles nodded. He understood, but that didn't make it any easier.

Seeing the gloomy look on the young cadet's face, Dr. Briggins offered a slight hope. "You might try one of the local funeral homes; there are two or three not too far away. Most of the morticians I know remove any gold teeth from the dead to give them to the family. You might have better luck there." Rising from the chair behind his desk, the dentist held out his hand. "Good luck, son. I hope you get your young lady that ring."

Charles had little hope of finding gold at a funeral chapel and was not surprised to find the first one locked without any answer. Telling himself that he would try one more suggestion given to him by Dr. Briggins before heading back to base, he was surprised when the mortuary door opened easily. He walked into a quiet room with hushed conversations going on in the room to his right. Seeing the woman seated and crying into a tissue, Charles hated to intrude upon any arrangements being made. Taking a seat close to the door, out of sight of the people in the meeting room, he closed his eyes and said a prayer for the people there, preparing to say goodbye for the final time to someone they loved.

Death was a constant companion in times of war, multiplied by the deliberate actions of battle. Such a sad and desperate time for families all over the world, Charles supposed. He thought of his mother and how she worried about him and his brother. He could only imagine how devastated she would be should one of them perish across the ocean in this cruel war. The letters he sent home with reassurances of their safety and God's will in their lives likely did little to calm her fears. The woman crying in the other room could well be his mother or could be Louise. Shaking his head, Charles focused on why he was here, trying to push aside the thoughts that lingered just at the edge of his consciousness every day.

There was a hallway on the other side of the waiting room, across from the occupied meeting room, and Charles nodded as an elderly woman entered.

"Hello there, young man. What can I do for you today?" The woman's voice was soft and caressing, like a mother to her child. The calm voice respected the arrangements in the meeting room, and Charles responded to her in the same quiet voice.

"Dr. Briggins, the dentist over on Cabal Street? He suggested I come here and talk to the mortician about some gold. You see, I would like to give my wife, well, she's not my wife yet, but she will be soon; I want to give her a nice wide, gold wedding band when we get married. But I need to find some gold," Charles began and stopped when the woman laid her hand on his shoulder.

"I see. Why don't you come back here and sit in Phillip's office? Phillip is my nephew. He'll be with you in a little bit of time, I think." She glanced over at the meeting room door. A soothing baritone voice could be heard.

Charles followed the woman down the hallway and into a small room with large windows overlooking an expanse of gently rolling hills dotted with graceful trees. Tombstones decorated the ground, reminding Charles again of life's fragility, especially in wartime.

Phillip Overton walked in a few minutes later, finding a young man staring out the windows. He walked over to the window and startled Charles in the same baritone voice that Charles had heard earlier. Lost in his thoughts, Charles didn't realize that anyone had entered, the footsteps quiet on the rugs on the floor.

"It is beautiful in its way, is it not? Peaceful. When I walk there sometimes early in the morning to clear my head, listening to the singing of the scrub jays and the coos of the mourning doves, I feel the peace that only God can provide. What can I do for you? My aunt said something about gold?" The mortician directed Charles to a set of chairs, each facing the other, realizing that he was not helping a relative deal with a family death.

Charles explained why he had come, mentioning that Dr. Briggins had suggested he try the area's funeral homes.

Phillip Overton nodded. "I know Briggins. Good man. Got a family plot out there," he said, nodding toward the window. The mortician studied the young soldier. With a strong chin and piercing eyes, the strength of purpose emanated from the tall man in front of him.

"Are you a praying man, Mr. Poag?" Overton surprised Charles with the question.

"Yes, sir. Probably not as much as I should, but praying is something my mother taught me a long time ago, and it's held me in good stead for these years. I think there's probably a lot of praying going up from lots of people with all that's going on in the world, the war, you know, and everything," Charles didn't know how to continue and was thankful that the mortician nodded, stopping him.

"Well, Mr. Poag, I was thinking this morning about what I should do with these gold teeth left here, and nobody seems to want them. I could sell them, for sure, and get a bit of extra money, but I prayed about it, you see. I had noticed that box of gold teeth and couldn't decide what to do with them. So I prayed on it," Overton repeated. "And here you are. Sounds like an answer to me; how about you?"

Charles couldn't believe his luck. Insisting that he pay, he exchanged what he was sure was a very low estimate of the worth of the gold in cash for the box of gold teeth and immediately headed over to the jeweler to have the gold turned into the wedding bands.

Phillip Overton looked up as his aunt joined him at the door to the funeral home, watching as Charles rushed to his car. "That Air Force boy is a good one," his aunt said.

"I believe you're right. Here," he said, giving her the cash Charles had pressed into his hands. "Put it in the basket at church."

May 11
Thursday night

Dear Mother, Dad & Joe,

Mother, I went down to the PX to try and buy you a Mother's Day card but they didn't have any so I don't guess I will send you one. But you know I think you are the best mother in the whole world and that I will think about you on Sunday, also every other day. I sure wish I could come home and eat dinner with you Sunday.

I haven't heard from Dalcomb in about 2 weeks. I guess he is up in South Dakota by now. I think he is pretty lucky in some ways. This stuff we have to go through sure gets on your nerves. I will sure be glad when Louise gets out here. I would feel lots better if I could just see anybody from home. It won't be long before I have been in this stuff for 8 months. In some ways it only seems like it has been a month and then in other ways it seems like 8 years since I left home.

I hope you and Dad are feeling alright now. I bet Dad has got a pretty garden. How is your little chickens getting along? I don't think a food shortage will bother you very much with all that food and just three people to eat it. I get good food here. We have milk every meal now.

Love, Charles

*May 15, 1944
Monday*

Dear Mother, Dad & Joe,

I have been pretty busy over the weekend. I got Louise a place to live this weekend. I got her a private room in a private home right on the beach. The folks she is going to stay with are about 50 years old and it is just a man and his wife in the whole house. They seem real nice and they are going to let Louise have kitchen privileges so she can cook her meals right there. I think she will like the place fine; it is right on the beach in a town named Balboa. It is about 5 miles from the base where I am. It cost me $8.00 per week. I think that is really cheap. Things out here are pretty high.

Mother, I thought about you all day yesterday. I sure wish I could have seen you on Mother's Day. I am having quite a bit of trouble with code. But I believe I will get it some way. It sure is hard for me. I just don't have any rhythm at all.

Dad, how is your garden doing? Have you got you any pigs? We have ham some time in the mess hall. I sure would like to have some good fried chicken and ham.

That's about all I know. Write me every time you can. I sure enjoyed Joe's letter. I wish he would write more often.

Love, Charles

The past few days had been different without Frank in the bunk next to him. He knew most of the men in his section and considered them all friends. But it was a loss, a loss of a confidant. He saw him occasionally on the base, but they no longer had duties posted together. Frank had agreed to be his best man if he didn't have guard duty.

Charles looked around the barracks. Supper, along with mail call, was only a few minutes away, and the men remaining in the barracks were sitting on their bunks talking or reading letters. Charles knew friendships were important in how they conquered their fears of the unknown ahead of them. It was simple to pick out the ones that didn't fare well in difficult situations. Those were also usually the ones that washed out early. It was unfortunate for those unable to form those bonds that helped bridge the gap that occurred when they left their family behind.

Grabbing the letters he had finished to his mother and Louise, he wanted to post them before supper and mail call. He hoped to have a letter from Louise; she would be starting to drive here in the next week or so, and he was anxious about her trip. She was putting up a brave front; that was his Louise, but he was worried, and he knew she was a little frightened at the prospect of being on the road by herself for so many days. They had talked about it several times; Charles didn't want her to make the trip alone. Louise insisted that she would be fine after being unable to find someone that could take time off to accompany her. Neither of them wanted to wait any longer, however. Her parents were unhappy about the trip, begging her to reconsider the timing. One or both of them could accompany her at a later time. Louise had told him over the phone that her refusal had led to some unpleasant moments, with her mother crying and her father visibly upset, asserting that nice young women didn't travel alone across the desert. Louise told Charles about that statement, laughing. She said she asked her father if it would be okay to travel alone across the mountains or the plains and avoid the desert. Assuring them that she would talk to them every day might be impossible, but she would certainly try. Charles knew he wouldn't sleep well until she was safely in the home he had found for her. His excitement at seeing her was tempered by his fears for her safe trip across the country. He hoped God was ready for a lot of messages coming His way.

As he left the barracks, the sounds from Shermie's bugle split the air. Shermie (so named because his mother claimed General Sherman was his great-grandfather) did his best on the bugle, but most of the notes were a little off, and it sounded more like a sick sheep bleating most of the time. Mess call was his best one, though, so the sounds didn't make you want to cover your ears. The bugle for mail call was about the same, but the other bugle calls were not pleasant. Shermie admitted that he wasn't very good at it, but he was all they had.

13

World War II

Although removed from the war-torn areas in Europe, families across the United States found themselves on edge each day as the battles continued. Trying to normalize the daily events that were usually celebrated, such as weddings, births, and birthdays, the concern for what was happening on the war front was never far from their thoughts.

Unknown to the families and most of the men on the battlefront, the Western Allies were preparing to deliver the greatest punch of the war. General Eisenhower, supreme commander of the operation code-named Overlord, was ready for the invasion of northern France. Twelve nations working together under Eisenhower's leadership would take on the German-occupied beaches of Normandy.

ND# California

Charles stared at the words in front of him. His eyes blurred from studying. Taking his gaze away from the papers on his desk, he looked across the empty room. Dalcomb was right. This coding stuff would drive you crazy. Being able to send and receive eight words a minute seemed to be an impossible aim. Encouragement from his brother and the other guys on base did little to raise his hopes. The continued 'once you get it, it's easy' didn't help when he didn't feel like he was getting it.

Frank had been in the chow line earlier, and Charles was able to talk to him for a few minutes before mail call. Frank, too, was having a hard time with coding, but that wasn't the only class he was struggling with. Frank told him he thought he would probably wash out in the next set of guys, and he seemed okay. When Charles asked him about Sherry, Frank only shrugged and left the mess hall before mail call. That could only mean he wasn't expecting a letter from Sherry, Charles assumed.

Charles' thoughts went to Dalcomb. His last letter from his brother said he didn't like Sioux Falls. Hopefully, it will get better. It was still hard to understand why Dalcomb washed out. Charles thought that if either of them washed out, he would be the one, not his brother.

Rubbing his eyes, he leaned back in the chair and closed them, telling himself he couldn't fall asleep. Smiling, he thought about Louise. She was on her way to him. A long trip, to be sure, but at least she was on her way. More praying. God, please keep her safe, he thought. He had talked to her once since she had left, prevailing upon her to stop each day before darkness settled on the highway. Her brother Jack had begun the trip with her but homesick for his girlfriend, Charlene, he had taken a bus back home, leaving Louise to continue alone to California.

He and Louise had another long conversation about their decision to get married. Thankfully, the officer's room was empty, and he could talk as long as he wanted. Charles wanted to blame it on last-minute jitters, but he knew it went deeper. The war would never be far from their thoughts. He didn't want to leave Louise a young war widow, but what promises could he give her? She assured him constantly that there was nowhere she wanted to be except with him, and he knew it to be true, but still. She owned his heart.

Charles had girlfriends in high school and some since, just as he knew, Louise had her share of boyfriends courting her. Charles had even imagined himself in love before and realized shortly after he met Louise that he had never known romantic love until she came into his life. How could he not want her to be his wife? His conversation with her always ended the same way. Louise always convinced him that getting married was right for both of them. Once he assured her that he never regretted asking her to be his wife and that he couldn't imagine life without her, she was adamant. Nothing he could say about the war changed anything in her mind. She wanted to be with him. He reminded himself of that again; his most fervent prayer was being answered. God would join them together. Forever.

Charles took a deep breath. Okay, just a short nap right here in the chair. Then a little more studying and a letter home. And no complaining, nothing that would cause his mother to worry. Not any more than she already did, anyway.

Tricia Cundiff

May 21, 1944

Dear Mother, Dad, & Joe,

Today has been a dreary day here. I went to Balboa last night and I have just been laying around most of the day. I sure am glad when Sunday comes so I can kindly rest up a little. They are sure putting us through the mill. We have so much to do in such a short time.

Well, mother, I guess Louise is on her way here. I sure wish you and Dad could have come out. I would sure like to have you at my wedding. I guess I will have a military wedding. I can get the same kind of wedding as an officer, since I am a cadet. I guess we will only have a few of my buddies. They have the organ play in the chapel and they have candles on the altar. The chaplain wears tails and everything is really nice and it don't cost one penny (that is what I like.)

I had a letter from Sarah and she said the baby was really growing and that he was sure a good baby. I sure wish I could have been with you on Mother's Day. Maybe this war will be over by this time next year. I sure hope so anyway.

I am glad Dad has got a good garden. I bet you really cook some good meals with fresh vegetables and plenty of fried chicken. We have good food here but they just don't know how to cook it. I sure hope Louise can learn to cook good like you. You are the best cook in this world.

Well, that's about all I know for now. Tell Joe he should see my suntan. I really am black on the face now. I don't look or feel like the same person that came in the Army 8 months ago.

Love, Charles

Love, Charles

Sunday night suppers were some of the best offered, and few of the men missed it. Charles had searched for Frank after supper, missing him in the mess hall. He had talked to a few men in Frank's barracks, and they didn't offer much. It didn't seem they knew him very well, only commenting that he kept to himself and they hadn't seen him all day.

The basketball court was his last stop. It was almost too dark to see the hoop, but he supposed Frank could be there. Glancing around the space, he almost missed the figure sitting on the ground to the side of the goal. Frank looked up blankly as Charles walked up and said, "Frank? What are you doing here? Are you okay? Are you sick?"

Frank shook his head and stood up. "Sure, Charley, I'm good. What's going on?"

Charles could tell Frank was not doing all that well and said so.

Frank shrugged. "Nothing you can do about it, man. I knew it before I ever changed barracks. I'm not making it in this program. They're shipping me off somewhere else; I don't know where yet. It's all good, though. I'll be okay wherever they send me. You'll be the one flying those bombers, Charley, my man. Drop some on those Japs for me, okay?"

Charles didn't know what to say. He had come to remind Frank that his wedding was coming up in less than a week, and he still wanted him to be his best man. "Oh, Frank, that's awful. I hate it. I wanted you and me to be up there together, chasing the clouds."

"Nah, you were always better at it than I was," Frank said, smiling. The smile didn't reach his eyes, though.

"Well, you'll still be here this weekend. I'm getting married! I need my best buddy to stand up with me," Charles asked.

"Oh, Charley, I can't do it. I'm sorry. I've got KP all day. You don't want me there anyway. I would be kind of a drip; everybody around should be happy on your wedding day.

Yeah, you and Louise, you want a happy man standing up there. I wouldn't be the one, trust me, Charley." Frank looked away.

"Frank. Tell me. I know this is bad. Washing out happens to a lot of the good guys, you know. I think most of it is luck. But there's something else, too. What's going on with Sherry?" Charles felt sorry that everyone couldn't be as happy as he was. With so much going on in the world, it was quite a lift to have something to look forward to and be excited about.

"Sherry. Ah, she's got some other guy now." Frank looked at Charles with a sad smile. "It's for the best, you know. She's there, and I'm here. Who knows where I'll be next?"

Charles studied his friend's face. "Frank. You're not alone, you know. Wherever you go, we're going to write and keep in touch. You're a part of my family, now, okay?"

"Sure we are, buddy. Wow, I guess I'm too late for mess, huh? I'm going to find me some food. I'll talk to you soon, Charley," Frank said, walking away from Charles as if he wanted to avoid any more conversation. Turning around and waving, he yelled, "Congratulations, Charley! Kiss that pretty lady for me!"

"Don't you leave without letting me know where you're going," Charles yelled, watching as Frank began to jog up the hill.

Okay, Charles thought, I need to ask one of the guys to stand up with me. Heading back to his barracks, he considered which of them he would ask. Tommy Peacock's wife would be one of the witnesses; Tommy couldn't stand with him because he had guard duty. Maybe Floyd could? He would ask Floyd Russell as soon as he saw him.

Charles found himself sitting on a wooden bench outside the first set of barracks. Frank was leaving. Charles knew he needed to find Floyd Russell, but he felt a real loss and concern for his friend. Frank had been with him since boot camp. Charles had friends back home and had made many friends here, but the rapport he and Frank had was almost immediate when they met. The late-night discussions about their girls, their hopes to fly, and even their fears about the future made the separation from friends and family back home easier to handle. There was a 'got your back' sense to buddies in the service. Charles had seen that most of the men, if they were lucky, developed that friendship in their training cycles; it helped to get through the difficult times.

Tricia Cundiff

14

California

'Today I'm getting married.' Charles repeated it to himself, looking into the small mirror over the basin. Saturday, June 3. This day will be my anniversary next year, he thought. Saturday, June 3. Maybe next year, he wouldn't be so nervous. Glancing down at his watch, Charles took a deep breath. Just a few more hours. He was leaving the single life behind and starting a new life. Maybe not how he had imagined it; it was hard to think about being married and not living with your wife. But there were lots of men doing it, he supposed. Most men he had come in contact with during his time in the Army were married, and the majority were recently married. A magazine article said that almost two million people were married in 1942 alone, mainly because of the war. Charles hoped all those couples would be as happy as he and Louise. No doubts were clouding his thoughts today. At the end of this day, he would be complete. Louise would be his wife.

The next few hours were quickly packed with work and preparing for his marriage. The time for the chaplain was set for 2:00, and Charles worked with his crew until he needed to leave to shower and change. Garbage detail was one factor he had not anticipated on his wedding day. Leaving the crew to continue with their garbage collections, Charles shrugged out of his jumpsuit, jumped in the shower, and put on his dress uniform. Looking into the mirror one last time before he hurried out, Charles bit his lip. Closing his eyes, he prayed. "God, I love this woman. I love her with everything I've got. If I shouldn't do this to her, if I'm going to leave her alone, oh God, I don't know. Stop me, I guess. Or maybe, just make my hands not shake so much." Opening his eyes, he straightened his tie and pulled his shoulders back. A calm settled, and he smiled. An answer. Or just plain love. He was getting married.

Louise was beautiful. His breath was taken away as he walked into the chapel to find her waiting at the altar for him. Straightening his tie again, realizing he was still nervous, he hurried to her and took her hands in his. The smile that met his melted away the anxious feelings.

"You ready for this?" his bride asked him.

"I've been ready for four years," he replied.

Charles barely noticed the flowers arranged throughout the small chapel, nodding at Floyd Russell, his best man. Floyd had agreed to stand with him and said he could use some pointers, as he was getting married soon.

The wedding vows were a blur; Charles couldn't concentrate on anything other than the eyes of the woman he was finally marrying. Her smile and misty eyes told him how happy she was. He had been concerned that she would be sad that her family and his couldn't be there, but his worry was chased away by the happiness in her gaze.

Holding her hand tightly as they left the chapel, Charles and Louise were surprised to find the crew Charles had left behind outside the doors forming a line. The men were cheering and holding up trash can lids to form an arch for the newly married couple to walk through. Louise laughed with the sheer joy of it, and Charles felt his heart swell. This was right. This was true. This was love.

June 4, 1944
Sunday night

Dear Mother, Dad & Joe,

Well, I guess you thought I had just about stopped writing. But I guess I have been pretty busy.

Mother, I am an old married man now. I got married yesterday at 2:00 p.m. in the chapel here on the base. I thought it was a real nice wedding and if I had it to do over I would want another just like this one. A Mrs. Peacock (a friend of mine's wife) was one of the witnesses and a fellow named Russell was my best man. It wasn't hardly anybody there. But the chapel had a lot of pretty white flowers and a lot of candles. The chaplain (Captain Gonser) married us then we had to kneel at the altar while he said a prayer.

I think the chapel looked as nice as any big church wedding with all the flowers and candles. Louise had a corsage of orchids (5 in a row). She really looked pretty I thought. She had a pretty blue dress and light shoes and a little hat of some kind. The lady she lives with cooked us a pretty cake. And we stayed down at the house last night. We went to Long Beach for our honeymoon (about 19 miles). This Army is funny. I only got off Saturday at 2:00 p.m. until Sunday 3:00 to get married, honeymoon and everything. Louise cooked breakfast this morning and she can cook pretty good. Mrs. Wilson (the lady she lives with) said she could cook good. I think she is practicing all week.

I had a letter from Dalcomb last week and he said he was starting back in code again. I also heard from Sarah; she said the baby was doing just fine.

Mother, I told Louise to write you and tell you all about the wedding and everything. We didn't get our picture taken because it was too crowded in town but we will get them taken maybe next week. The only picture I have of Louise is a big eight by ten. If you want to let them use that to put in the Herald it is all right just tell them that is all you have and I guess they make any size they want to go in the paper.

Love, Charles

Mr. and Mrs. J. F. Ramsay

announce the marriage of their daughter

Louise

to

Charles H. Poag

United States Army Air Forces

on Saturday, the third of June

Nineteen hundred and forty-four

Santa Ana, California

World War II

June 6, 1944, D-Day, would end with the Allies established on the shore and providing the means to advancement into France. Beaches stretching fifty miles along the coast of Normandy were the targets. Five beaches with code names Utah, Omaha, Gold, Juno, and Sword, were the landing sites for ground troops sent to liberate northwest Europe from the Nazis.

Omaha Beach endured the most casualties of war, and as news spread of the Allies' victories, families worldwide celebrated and feared the worst, waiting for news of their sons. With over two thousand American men killed on Omaha Beach alone, casualties of war numbers increased substantially. Many family members were left with nothing but a memory of the son they saw leave for war; many soldiers were killed and swept out to sea during the battle.

American mothers and mothers across the globe knelt in prayer for the safe return of their sons, and women prayed for their husbands, grieved at their loss, or released a long-held breath of relief at the good news that their loved one was alive. The waiting for news was horrendous, with most families not aware of their soldier's location until after reports had been distributed and loved ones were notified.

California

June 10, 1944
Sunday

Dear Mother, Dad & Joe,

Well, mother, I guess I will be ready to leave here pretty soon if I pass everything. I take all my final tests next week and I believe I will be out of here by the 1st of July. I will kindly be glad to start flying again. But I hope I can find Louise a nice place to live when I move. We sure have got a nice place here. Louise really likes the lady she lives with. She is real nice to us and she really likes to talk to Louise. I guess Louise will stay there until I get moved and find her a place to stay.

I had a letter from Mike and he said he was doing fine and saving a lot of money. I think he is going to buy a farm with about 550 acres of land. I bet he really gets a good start if he don't have to go to the Army, and I sure hope he doesn't.

Dad, what do you think about the war now? I believe Germany will be whipped before this winter and after they are out of the way it won't take long to whip Japan. I believe this time next year it will all be over or pretty close to it anyway.

We went up to Hollywood last night and looked all over the place. We saw all the big broadcasting stations. NBC and CBS and also all the big night clubs. We drove through Beverly Hills where all the movie actors live, and also went to the Hollywood canteen. I don't care much for all that stuff, it looks just like any other place to me.

Mother, I don't know if I told you or not but I am a cadet officer now and I have about 2000 men under me. I am wing staff member and I don't have to do any more details like KP or guard, etc. I have to inspect barracks and men and I sure do hate to gig them. I don't like to pass out gigs because I hate to see those fellows walk tours. I don't know why I was selected for this job. It is the highest thing you can be here. So I feel like it is a honor anyway.

I had a letter from Dalcomb. I think he is liking Sioux Falls better now. I believe he will really make good in radio.

Love, Charles

Louise looked over his shoulder, reading the letter he had written. Each of them usually wrote their parents after Charles returned to the base on Sunday night, but this morning turned into a lazy day after a busy one in Hollywood and Beverly Hills the day before.

"Did I leave anything out?" Charles asked her.

"No, I think you covered it," Louise said as she wrapped her arms around his neck from behind. Charles turned in the chair next to the small desk in Louise's room, pulling her onto his lap.

Smiling, he asked, "Have I told you today that you're the prettiest girl in the world?"

"I don't think so, and I think you're crazy, but I'm glad you think so. Have I told you how very proud I am of you?" Louise said as she looked into his eyes, and he felt the pangs of love again take his breath away.

"Proud of me? Dumb ole' me? Whatever for, pretty lady?" Charles grinned at the woman who owned his heart.

"You care. You care about your family. You care about the men you supervise. You care about the war. I think you care very deeply."

Charles shrugged. "Of course, I care. Anybody would. I do what I'm told, sweetheart. I hate this war. I hate what it is doing to us, to the men, to the whole world. But bad stuff has to be swept away. I heard we're making progress; we landed in Normandy and will take back Europe. Hitler won't win this. You've heard. Then we take care of Japan and that lunatic. Somehow we are going to do this; we have to."

Louise lowered her voice so that her landlords couldn't hear. "Mr. Wilson said that many of our boys died when they took the beaches over there. They've friends who haven't heard back from their son in over three weeks. I think they expect the worst." She stood and walked over to the window overlooking the small backyard.

"Enough," Charles said, walking over and pulling her against him. "We have better things to talk about. Like, say, what kind of place do you want me to look for when they move me?"

Louise nodded. "You're right. We can't fix the war." She turned and faced him, running her fingers through his hair, pushing it back from his forehead. "I suppose we should wait until we know where you're going next before we decide where I'll live. I can start looking when you get your orders. You don't have to do all this by yourself anymore."

"But I want to take care of you. I don't even want you to work, but I guess you have to," Charles said, shaking his head.

"Chaz, don't be silly. I want to work. What would I do with my time? Besides, anything we can save will help down the road, don't you think?"

Charles smiled and pulled her closer. "How did I get so lucky to get such a smart wife?"

"No luck. You just knew the right people," Louise answered, grinning.

"Right. It's always who you know. And I knew Avery. Dear old Avery Green. I owe him a bundle. A lot more than the hundred dollars he won't let me forget about."

Charles could see the Wilsons, Louise's landlords, getting into their car. "Where are the Wilsons going?" Charles asked.

"I told them we might not go to church this morning since we would be late getting in last night. Mrs. Wilson said they were going to visit some friends after lunch. I suppose that's where they're headed," Louise said, glancing out the window as the '40 Ford sedan backed out of the short driveway.

"I didn't even hear them when they left for church this morning," Charles said, shaking his head.

"I guess not, with all the snoring you were doing," Louise replied.

"Oh, my sweetie, I'm sorry. Did I keep you awake?" Charles looked at her, concerned.

"No, no, Chaz. I didn't mean that. It's a comforting sound. I sleep much better when you're here," Louise said, smiling tenderly.

Charles sighed. He was so lucky. "I'll have to leave soon; I need to do a barracks check before the recruits get assigned." He looked down at his watch. "I only have a couple of hours. What do you want to do?"

"Let me think," Louise said, mischievously placing her finger on her forehead. "Oh, I thought of something!"

It was a small room, not far to the bed, freshly made up only a couple of hours before.

June 16, 1944
Friday night

Dear Mother, Dad, & Joe-

I am feeling pretty good tonight. I just got through taking all my final tests today and I passed everything fine, even code. I sure had a time with code but I had an average of over 90 in all my other subjects; they were pretty easy. I guess I will be leaving here in about 2 weeks. I don't know where I will be sent or even when I will leave. But I just think I will be leaving pretty soon. I sure will be glad when I start flying. I really like flying. We will be flying lots bigger planes and it will be lots more fun. The planes we fly in primary are open cockpits and you can do loops, spins, and all kinds of stunts in them.

Well, Louise hasn't left me yet so I guess she is going to try and live with me for a while. I sure do feel lots better about this whole Army now. I at least have something to look forward to over the weekends. I think it will help to make the time pass a little faster. I am sure lots happier and I think Louise will make me a good wife. She can cook pretty good.

Dad, what do you think of the war situation now? I believe this war will be over by the first of next year. I don't believe Germany can hold out until this winter, do you?

That sure was a good price you were offered for your car. If you could get by without a car it would be a good price. But I wouldn't buy any house now because I think they will be lots cheaper after the war. I would just use my own judgment about selling the car. It will be unhandy to get around without a car. But $900 is about all the car cost new.

Well, I got to go to bed. I will try and write a little more often.

Love, Charles

June 20, 1944

Dear Mother, Dad & Joe,

Well, I thought I had better drop you a line and tell you I will be leaving here next week and for you not to write me until I send you my new address.

Love, Charles

Mother, I don't think I ever thanked you for the pajamas you sent me. But I really thought they were nice and I slept the first night of my married life in them. Mother, I don't want you to get Louise and I anything while I am in the Army because Louise has all the stuff she can carry around now. Mother, you have already done more for me than anybody. So don't buy up anything for me. I know I have the best mother and Dad in this whole world. I sure will be glad when this war Is over so I can come home. I don't think I will ever leave Tennessee again. It is so dry out here that they have to water the weeds to make them grow.

Louise and I are getting along just fine. I hate for her to have to move again but I guess she will get used to that if she stays with me. She will probably get a job when we get moved.

Mother, I had my insurance changed. I left $5000 to you and $5000 for Louise. I want you to have that much anyway. I am planning coming back all right but it is nice to have if I don't.

I will send you my new address just as soon as I get moved.

Love, Charles

Charles felt fortunate that he could reach Louise by phone during the week. Phones were still a luxury many couldn't afford, and he and Louise were both thankful that her landlords, the Wilsons, had decided to have one installed.

Regarding their telephone use, Charles rarely called Louise during the week, limiting their calls to once or twice a week. He hated to call a third time, but it was too important to wait.

"Hello, Mrs. Wilson? I'm so sorry to bother you again. May I speak to Louise, please? It's very important. I'm sure she'll tell you about it after we finish. I'll only keep her a couple of minutes," Charles asked when the phone was answered.

A short couple of minutes later, Louise answered hesitantly. "Chaz? Is everything okay?"

"Yes, oh yes, my sweetie. Louise, I just got my orders. We're going to Phoenix. Phoenix! Well, it's Scottsdale, but it's a Phoenix address. I'm going to the Thunderbird Field; it's listed as Field two. I thought it might be Texas, close to San Antonio, but it's not. It's Phoenix. At least it's not too far from here. Not as far as San Antonio, anyway. Louise? You there?" Charles hesitated.

"Oh yes, everything is good. It's great, Chaz. I was so scared! I thought it was something terrible you were calling me about. I'll see you tomorrow! It's okay; I'm glad you called. Phoenix? We talked about Phoenix. That's good. A day away. That will make it easier to find a place to stay." Louise sounded relieved.

"Oh, baby, I'm so sorry. I didn't mean to scare you. I just wanted to share it with you. I wanted you to know as soon as I did. It's where we'll be next. Together, you know. Okay. I'll see you tomorrow. I love you, Louise," Charles said softly.

"I love you, too, Chaz. Tomorrow. Bye, now."

Charles heard her voice and sighed. It would be hard to leave her if this war kept on and he was sent overseas. He shook his head. No use worrying over that now, he thought. God will take care of everything. His mother told him that. He trusted his mother. He trusted God.

15

Arizona

June 29, 1944
Thursday

Dear Mother, Dad & Joe,

Well, here I am on the desert. In the winter time they send me up north, and in the summer they send me to the desert. I guess I will be used to most all kinds of climate when I get home.

Mother, I got here Wednesday morning; this field is about 20 miles from Phoenix right out here in 'Paradise Valley.' That is what it is called. I think it is 'desert valley.' It is pretty hot here; it was above 100 degrees yesterday and everybody thought it was a cool day. It usually gets about 120 to 135 in the shade and it isn't a tree in sight.

Louise came out and got here Wednesday also. She has already got her a place to live in Phoenix. She got a nice room, 'airconditioned' with board. She is going to see about getting a job today, I think. I am quarantined for 2 weeks. But I called Louise last night and she had already got here and had the room. Another fellow's wife came with her. I guess I can travel with her from here on until I finish this training.

Mother, this field is sure pretty. We have cottages with 10 men to a room. The barracks are all 'air conditioned,' as well as the mess hall, recreation hall, etc. We have a swimming pool right in the center of the barracks. It really gets cold at night. You have to sleep under a blanket after 12:00 at night. So it isn't so bad after all. It's only about 400 men here, and they sure have a lot of airplanes. We were issued our helmets and goggles this morning. So I guess we will start flying tomorrow or Saturday.

They wash a lot of fellows out here. I guess I will find out if I can fly or not. A lot of people just can't fly so I may be one of them. But I am not going to worry about that. I believe I can fly the thing as well as anybody else. These planes are lots bigger than the cubs we flew. These planes have open cockpits also.

We get out of here on Saturday afternoon until Sunday night so I will have a little more time to be with my wife. I like this place just fine and I think Louise likes it alright also. I don't guess you would know us now. We are both brown and my hair is only ½ inch long all over. That's the way you have to wear it on this post. We don't have to wear ties here either; that's pretty nice. I sure hate to wear a tie all the time.

Dad, this is pretty country out here. Not a tree anywhere and they have cactus 10 feet high. The land is all pretty level. It sure gets hot however it is such a dry hot that you don't hurt like at home. You sweat all day but it dries so fast you don't even get your shirt wet.

Well, that's about all I know. Write me when you can. We had our pictures made and I guess Louise will send you one just as soon as we get them.

Love, Charles

"I know you love it. I'm just not sure I want to know when you're going to go up and how long you will be up there. It scares me, Chaz. I know it's silly. I know you're a good pilot. You're good at everything you do," Louise said, shaking her head.

"Sweetheart, I've told you over and over again. I'm safer up there than I am in a car. Every time I go up." Charles pulled Louise to him and rested his head on top of hers.

"I know that. I know that in my head, but I can't make it reach my heart. And I can't help it, Chaz, when I think about you flying, I start thinking about you flying over there with all the bombs, and what do you call them? Oh yeah, the dog fights? My head can get around it, but my heart can't." Louise had tears in her eyes; her voice was muffled as she leaned into Charles' chest.

Charles pulled back and tilted her head back. "We talked about this before I ever enlisted. You know, remember when we were talking about me being a pilot right after I got my orders? What was it that girl, you know, the waitress said at the diner? She said it was glamorous. Being a pilot and all. I thought you kind of agreed with her."

"Of course, I agreed with her. Being a pilot is what you want. And I want what you want. It's still frightening, especially in war. I think I would be okay and not get so anxious after a few years, anyway, if you were flying planes here. But over there? My head aches just thinking about it. The days that I know you're in the air? Those are the days I feel like I can't breathe. And then it's night, and I haven't heard anything, or you call, and I know you're okay," Louise ran the words together as if she had been holding them in much too long.

"Oh, Louise, I had no idea you were this upset about it! We've talked about this before; I don't know how to reassure you about it any more than I've already tried to," Charles shook his head, looking down at her and seeing her fear.

Turning away from his embrace, Louise wiped her teary eyes. "It's okay; I'll get used to it, I know. After the war. But now? I hear so many things, Chaz, so many horrifying things."

Charles looked down at his watch. "I hate to leave you like this. I'm due back at the base in just over an hour; I've got to go." Walking his wife over to the small chair in her room, he placed her in his lap and pulled her willing head onto his shoulder. "How about this? Don't worry about me, and I'll tell you about the flight afterward. No more which days I'll be in the air?"

Louise laughed despite the fear she couldn't let go of. "So, I'll just think about you being in the air every day. No, Charles Poag, that's worse. I need to know so I can pray you down," she said, taking the tissue Charles offered her and wiping her nose.

"Look at it this way, Louise. I'm probably going to wash out. The guys say that everybody is going to, and they're going to shut this place down. So you might get what you want, and I'll be done flying," Charles said, looking away from her.

"That's not what I want! You know that. I want you to be a pilot. I know it's what you want, and I do so want you to be happy," Louise replied, using a finger to turn his head back towards her.

Charles smiled a lopsided grin. "I know you support me. Tell you what. Let's just let God take care of this. It'll be what He wants; that's what we want, huh?" He hugged her as she nodded. He continued, "And I want you to be happy. This job, it's still good? You think you're going to like it?"

"Sure I am. No more talking. You've got to leave soon," Louise said, lifting her face to his.

Love, Charles

July 7, 1944
Friday night

Dear Mother, Dad & Joe,

Well, I am still flying and haven't killed myself yet. I guess I will solo the first of next week. I guess it will feel pretty funny flying around by myself for a while. Mother, I don't want you and Dad worrying about me. These airplanes are no more dangerous than a car if you know how to fly them. I really like this flying. I just hope I don't wash out and go on and finish this training.

I wish Dalcomb wouldn't worry about being in this Army. He thinks he has ruined his life, well, what do you think about me? Just when I started making a little money I had to get in. There are 12,000,000 other men in here and they all think the same thing. I think we should be thankful that we are still over here and not over there fighting already. I don't like this war at all but we have to be in it.

I fly about one hour a day and we have to take PT and run from one to three miles everyday. It was pretty hard at first but I am about used to it now.

I don't get out again this weekend, so I guess Louise will come out to see me Saturday night for a while. She really likes her place and also her job.

Mother, I had a picture made by my airplane; I will send you one just as soon as I have time.

They sure do keep us busy here. You never had any time for anything.

Mother, tell Joe I want him to get me some gas coupons and send me some if he possibly can. We are short of gas and I want a little extra gas. Tell him if he will keep me in gas until Christmas, I will be home and I will take him up and let him fly and I will do some spins, loops and snap rolls.

I sure would like to be at Armour now. I have been to a lot of places but I had rather live at Armour than any place in Arizona. I am going to try and buy one of those little two room houses after I get home and just live there all my life.

Tell Joe if he don't send me plenty of gas coupons and write me some time I am going to beat heck out of him. I also want a Kodak picture of him. He is the only one of the family I haven't got a picture of.

Love, Charles

World War II

World War II was different from previous wars in that information was readily available to the public through new media sources. While most Americans followed news of the war through radio and newspapers, newsreels that preceded movies at theaters provided additional visual information from the war front. With many correspondents placed close to the front lines, information was sent that was closely edited by the military. The creation of a military office of censorship was deemed necessary, and if the press wanted access, they had to apply for credentials from this office. This meant that the media applying for access had to play ball with the military. This agreement kept information like the creation of the a-bomb out of the press until after the war.

The media industry, acknowledging its importance in distributing information to the American people, envisioned its role as supporting the war effort and promoting nationalism throughout the country.

Arizona

"Hi, sweetheart. I hope it's okay I called you this late," Charles said, holding the phone close to his ear. The clerk was standing only a few feet away, and while the young man looked busy, Charles knew he could probably hear everything he said.

"It's not late, Chaz. It's only about seven. Is everything okay?" Louise had been startled when her name had been yelled out from down the hall about a phone call. She had talked to Chaz last night; it was unusual for him to call this soon.

"Yeah, yeah. I'm okay. Just needed to talk to you, that's all. I know you don't want to hear about me flying, but it's been a rough one today," Charles began, hesitating when Louise spoke.

"No, baby. Don't say that. I know I said that I didn't want to hear about it, but that was just me giving in to being afraid. I don't want it like that. I want to hear everything about your day, everything about what you're doing. Tell me, Chaz, I'm right here, just a phone call away. I'll always be here." Louise was speaking too fast; she knew it, but she couldn't let down the man she loved with all her heart.

"It's just exhausting, Louise. Standing on the flight line for hours, I get to fly for one hour and then it's back on the line. And I don't know if I'll ever be able to fly like they want me to. The whole program is getting tough. I hear that it is almost impossible to get through it now. They just don't need pilots anymore, so they're washing out everybody. I think I've wasted so much time with this, Louise, and I feel so stuck." Charles let out a long sigh, glancing over at the clerk.

"Oh, Chaz. I'm sure it's not that bad. You're tired. Did you get to solo? I know you wanted to. How did that go?" Louise wished she could be with him. It was hard, this being married and not being together. She couldn't even imagine how it would be if Chaz had to go overseas.

"Good, I think. It felt funny flying up there alone, but I wasn't scared at all. I landed three times and made some good landings. I'll solo again next week, I think," Charles answered. "I didn't want to scare you, Louise. I just needed to hear your voice, I think. I'll get out Saturday around one, and I don't have to be back on base until Sunday night at nine. Seeing you is what I need. Oh yeah, I got a letter from Mother. Joe is sending us some gas coupons. That'll help. Maybe I'll get them before Saturday, and I'll bring them. I'll bring the letters from Sarah and Dalcomb so you can read them. Sarah sent me some pictures of our nephew. He's a cute kid."

Louise sighed. He sounded better than he had when she first answered the phone. He needed someone to talk to, she thought, and I'm glad I'm the one he needed. "I can hardly wait. Weekends are what makes the rest worth it, you know. Maybe we can go somewhere and get Baby Michael something."

"That sounds good. Thank you, sweetheart, for listening to this dumb guy. I think I just miss you, that's all," Charles said, realizing that he did feel much better in just the few minutes he had been on the phone with Louise.

The clerk smiled as Charles and Louise completed their phone call, words of love and promises ending the conversation. Charles looked at the clerk as he left, an unnecessary salute accompanying the smile that followed him out the door.

July 25, 1944

Dear Mother, Dad & Joe,

I am still flying everyday. I sure do like this flying; it is a lot of fun but sure is a lot of work, too. I guess I am doing alright; I have 26 hours of flying now. I get to take a plane up by myself all the time.

Well, I got off last Friday night at 7:00 and didn't have to come back until Sunday night. That was the longest time I had been with my wife since I was married. They let the best flight out on Friday night so we won last week but I don't guess we will get that again for a while.

Mother, you asked if I was making any more money now. Yes, I am, I make $103.00 per month since I got married. Louise gets $50.00 a month and I usually draw about $40 or $45 after they take out for everything. I don't have to pay any insurance while I am flying. The government pays it for me. Louise draws about $35 per week from her job so we are saving a little bit of money now but it costs quite a bit to move around and do anything over the weekends. I think we will be able to get by just fine until I can finish this course alright if I don't wash out.

I hope Joe can get a few stamps but I don't want him to cut yourself short any. Louise has to drive the car to work and it takes at least 2 gallons a week for that. I don't have any connections out here. So it is kindly hard to have any gas to do anything with Louise on the weekend.

Tell Joe I still want a picture of him and I sure wish he would write me and tell me how he likes his work and what he is doing. I don't think he even realizes he has a brother!

Love, Charles

Mother, some time when you cook a cake or cookies how about sending me a piece. I still have never found anybody who could stay in the race with your cooking.

I will try and write a little more often. I believe this war will be over pretty soon now.

Love, Charles

Tricia Cundiff

16

Arizona

"Look! Another one!" Astride a large white Arabian, Louise pointed across the slight rise on the path in front of them. The horse was not disturbed by the large rabbit standing on its hind legs staring at them.

"Yeah, they seem to be everywhere. The horses aren't bothered, so I guess it's commonplace around here," Charles answered as he viewed the quiet beauty surrounding them. Besides the sounds of their voices and the occasional snort of the horses as they anticipated a gallop, the desert was silent. A light breeze ruffled Louise's hair; he smiled at the picture she made sitting on the horse, her face glowing with contentment. This is what they needed, a break from what had become the norm. The war seemed far away.

The desert sky was an amazing blue, with the occasional desert flower dotting the landscape. The mountains only a short distance away, he and Louise were bound for a trail leading them through the rock formations in the hills so they could view the valley from above.

Only a short drive from Phoenix, the stables were a welcome retreat. The wrangler had given him a beautiful stocky spotted Arabian while Louise sat on the white horse. Pulling up beside

Louise as she awarded him the smile he received as a gift, he patted the Arabian's head. "Tapper. That's kind of a strange name, don't you think?"

Louise leaned down and hugged the white horse she sat upon. "Well, Sassy here knows why she has her name, don't you, girl?"

"I suppose so; she is a little fidgety. Tapper here waits patiently for me to let him go. How about it? Let's follow the jackrabbit. He seems to know where he's going."

Louise laughed. "Okay, just as long as you don't get us lost. We're supposed to stay on the trail."

"We won't leave the trail. The rabbit, look. He's following the trail, too," Charles said, nodding toward the rabbit loping through the rocks.

The towering cactus and rocky terrain didn't impede the horses, obviously accustomed to the trail and unlikely to stray from it, despite the occasional quail darting across the path. An hour later brought Charles and Louise to a view neither would have suspected awaited them.

Minutes passed as they inhaled the beauty before them. The barren landscape of sand, dotted with cactus and wind-torn rock formations, lay in front of them, rippled with shades of brown and burnt orange. The desert flowers they had seen on their way up the mountain were invisible against the starkness of the harsh sunlight.

Charles looked over at his wife. Her profile, with the intensity of her gaze upon the majestic valley below them, was a picture he would carry with him. The sunlight touched her face, wisps of hair blowing around her eyes; she raised her hand to push it away and looked over at him. The smile again, the smile that set his heart beating faster.

"The rocks," she said. "They're incredible. Look how they seem to move in the sun. It's so beautiful."

"You're the beautiful one. These rocks couldn't come close to how beautiful you are," Charles said to his bride.

"You're silly. Looking at me when you have all of this in front of you!" Louise shook her head, grinning.

"Maybe, but you're the hottest rock I've seen around here," he said, reaching over and placing his hand behind her head.

Laughing, she clasped his hand in hers. "That's me all right, a hot rock. Chaz, you're so silly."

"Yep, that's you. Hot Rock."

Only her laugh could beat that smile.

July 31, 1944

Dear Mother, Dad & Joe,

I received the nice letter from you last week and I sure was glad to get those stamps. Tell Joe I will take him for a nice long ride when I get home. I guess this gas will last me for a while but you tell old Joe if he gets a hold of any extra coupons not to forget me.

I am going alright with my flying. I have 20 hours now and I fly 2:30 hours by myself and then 45 minutes with my instructor. I have to take my 20 hour check ride with a lieutenant some time this week.

Louise is still working everyday. I guess she gets kindly homesick but she won't admit it. She sure is a game girl and she is doing a good job looking out for herself.

Mother, it really is hot out here. It stays about 110 degrees all the time. You never hear of anybody having a sun stroke out here. We take PT every day right out in the sun. We have to run from one to four miles every day. This heat doesn't hurt you much after you get used to it. This climate is really good for sinus trouble. It is dry as a powder house. It never rains and they have to irrigate to raise anything.

They sure do have a lot of pretty orange groves and grapefruit trees.

Louise and I went horseback riding yesterday. And we rode all around on the desert and up on the mountains. You can see these long-eared jackrabbits everywhere.

Love, Charles

"Have you been listening to the radio? I think this guy Dewey has a chance," Charles said, forcing another bite of his mother's cake into his mouth. He was full but couldn't resist. It was all he could do to keep the other men in his barracks from grabbing all that was left. He had brought the rest of the package of cakes to Louise's room, and told her to take some to work with her.

Louise smiled. Nibbling at the small piece of cake on her napkin, she nodded. "I guess so. There are a lot of people that think that Roosevelt has done a good job, though, with the war. The girls at work hear the same thing I do. They say we're winning the war, so Roosevelt might get it again."

"Maybe. I hope not. I think it's time to give someone else the top spot. Roosevelt's been there a long time, and he looks sick, you know?" Charles finished his second piece of cake and wiped his mouth with the cloth Louise had handed him. "All gone?" he asked, knowing that icing had a way of sticking to him as he gobbled it up.

Louise reached over and took the cloth, rubbing the side of his cheek. "You're a messy eater, Chaz."

"Ah, not so much. Only with the really good stuff," he replied. Taking a deep breath, he reached over for Louise's hand. "I need to tell you something," he began.

Noticing the serious tone, Louise laid down her fork, pushing the barely touched piece of cake over to the side of the small table in her room. "Okay," she said nervously.

"No, nothing bad. Well, a little bad for me, but I'm not sure you'll be sad about it," Charles said.

"Enough! What is it, Chaz? What's so wrong?" Louise wasn't sure what was coming next.

"It's just that I don't think I will make it. Being a pilot, I mean. They're washing everybody out almost. I failed my check ride. That's not so bad; everybody who takes a check ride fails it now. They just don't need any more pilots. They are making it so tough you just can't make it," Charles looked past her eyes to the wall, shaking his head.

"But you've worked so hard! All that studying and no sleep. It's not fair, Chaz! Are you sure? Can they really do that?" Louise hated to see the disappointment on her husband's face.

"It's not done yet, but if I fail my recheck, I'll be out. It's okay; I think you'll be just a little bit relieved, right? Maybe I will, too."

Louise shook her head. "Don't say that. It's not over yet, Chaz. I want this for you because you want this. You just have to put up with my silly worrying, just like your mother's. We worry because we love you and want you to be safe and come home."

"I know, I know. But I wanted you to be prepared. It won't be a bad thing if I wash out, Louise. I can probably get into airplane mechanic's school. I would probably get a furlough, maybe a decent one where we could go home for a few days. I wrote Mother and told her I was probably going to wash out, so she's probably hoping I do." Charles shrugged.

"Now that's just silly. Your mother hopes no such thing. She wants you to have what you want, just like I do." Louise reached over and pulled Charles to her, wrapping her arms around his neck. "It's okay to be a little down, but don't give up. We pray for God's will always. If God wants you up in those skies for the Army, that's where you'll be!"

"That's what I told Mother." He leaned back to look into his wife's eyes. "Enough of that. I wanted to prepare you, that's all. We'll probably be moving again. I know that you're thrilled about that."

"One place at a time, Chaz. I go where you go, if at all possible. Remember that. We're better together, always," Louise said as she reached up and kissed him.

"Okay, Hot Rock. Let's get together," he said, laughing as he reached down and picked her up.

Cuddling together later, appreciative of the air-conditioning in Louise's room, Charles played with a tendril of hair that had escaped from behind her ear. "I've got a friend who'll get us some gas tomorrow. We can drive down to Mexico and check it out, stay somewhere and come back on Sunday morning. What do you think?"

"Why, Mr. Poag. Are you taking me away from all this?" Louise laughed as she spread her arms to include the small room they were in.

"I believe I will. If we weren't already married, I'd probably drag you to the chapel, and we'd get married, so all of this, uh, you know, would be legal and all that," Charles stumbled over his words, laughing.

"Aren't you glad we've got that part done?" Louise flirted.

"Yes, ma'am. I believe I am. And yes, I'm taking you away from all this; you will be with me wherever I go if there's any way I can make that happen," Charles replied.

"I don't think you'll have an unwilling partner," Louise said as she kissed him deeply. "Tomorrow, we go to Mexico for a day. But not tonight."

17

Arizona

August 16, 1944

Dear Mother, Dad & Joe,

Well, I thought I would drop you a line to let you know that I am no more a cadet. I washed out today. I knew it was coming sooner or later, but I just didn't know when. I am sure glad to get out. I thought I would hate to wash out but instead I don't mind at all. They just don't need any more pilots and they are just washing out everybody. We only have 10 men left in my flight and I guess they will get them in another week. The lieutenant that washed me said I was a good flier but the Army had just raised the standards so high that only about 10% of the men could get through.

I guess I will go to airplane mechanic school, that is what I want anyway. I have just had so much work and worry in this cadet training that it will be a relief to get back in the regular Army. I guess I will leave here in about 2 weeks and will be sent to Amarillo, Texas. That is at least closer to home.

I think Louise is glad I washed out, too. Because I can probably be with her more and she worried as much as I did about getting through.

Tell Dad we had a talk with a captain today and he said the war was so near over and they had such a reserve of pilots that they didn't want any more. They are closing this school the first of October, so they are just getting rid of all the cadets.

Mother, I don't want you to worry about me washing out. I asked God to let me do what was best and so I know this is for the best. It takes five months to get through airplane mechanic school and then the war will be over.

I got enough time here to get a civilian pilot license so tell Joe I will still take him riding when I get home and get my licenses.

I may be able to travel with Louise in the car for awhile now; I hope so anyway. Louise is going to move with me. She can probably get a job in Amarillo and I may be able to stay with her every night.

Love, Charles

"It's a good letter, Chaz," Louise said, handing it back to him. "But you're wrong about me being happy that you washed out. I want what you want, and I know how much you wanted that," she said as she ran her fingers through his hair.

"We both wanted what God wanted, right? So, we got what's best. That's all. That's behind us. It was a great experience, and hey, I got the hours. Flying will still be a part of my life," he said, reaching up to take her hand into his.

"You can write your folks, too. Mother will let Sarah know and anybody else that needs to find out. I wrote Dalcomb and told him. Tell your family that we'll have a new address later. I think we'll probably get home for a few days before we go to Amarillo," Charles said.

"I hope so. I know I have a big crew back home, but I do miss them. They can be overwhelming, so be prepared. They'll probably gang up on you now that we're married," Louise said, laughing.

"Jack's okay. He knows firsthand how much I love you. And your mom and dad? All good there. I'll need to make sure I get all the names right. Curry, Elizabeth, and Judy, they all know what a great guy I am, right?" Charles said, grinning. "You did tell them, didn't you?"

"I'm pretty sure I told them," Louise said, laughing.

"Has Judy heard back from Frost yet? He's been overseas, what, a year now? I thought they came home more often than that. "I know she's missing having her husband around," he said, clasping her hand in his.

Louise shrugged. "She had received one letter the last time I talked to her. Yes, she misses him a lot. And she really likes you, too. They all love you, I promise. You're right; I need to get busy writing letters home. Then I can send a short one when we know if we can visit before Texas." Louise put her arms around Charles' neck. "Oh baby, I'm sorry you didn't get what you wanted out here, but I think it's all going to be okay. Texas is another adventure, right?"

"It's all an adventure as long as I'm with you," Charles replied, pulling her closer.

World War II

News continued to trickle in of battles continuing in Europe. Against the advice of his commanders, Hitler ordered the advancement of his troops into Normandy, desiring to assault the Allies in response to their victories during Operation Cobra and the Normandy invasion. With no chance of success, the Germans were outflanked to the south and east, leading to the entrapment of the remaining German troops in the area.

General George Patton had rapidly advanced south and southeast after the battles of Normandy, and the Germans had little success breaking through the Allied soldiers' lines. Approximately fifty thousand Germans were trapped. Although some escaped, the losses to the German forces of men and equipment were significant.

American families, as well as Allied families across the globe, celebrated each success, although the news was frequently several weeks old. Soldiers on both sides of the ocean spoke of the end of the war and assured families back home the end was near.

The news came from the Central Pacific operations that American and Allied forces had progressed in their campaign to recapture the Philippines from the Japanese. The US Navy captured the Mariana and Palau Islands during the summer of 1944, intending to build air bases within range of the new B-29 bomber aimed at Japan's industrial cities.

Fighting a war on two fronts gave the news media an abundance of opportunities to provide American families with incentives for patriotism. Pamphlets were spread throughout small towns and cities, advocating rationing and supporting our troops. Parades were held around training bases in the United States, and victory news traveled quickly. Little was told of the horrors of war, the censorship machine in full force.

Word spread through the families of returning soldiers of the torture inflicted by the Germans and Japanese, and many were pushing for an end to the atrocities of war and celebrating each victory over the enemy. Mothers and wives prayed for the safe return of their men, filled with fear from the whisperings passed through the military families' grapevine.

The atrocities of the war against Jews were whispered throughout the Allied nations since the early battles in World War II. American newspapers reported that two million Jews had been murdered as early as the fall of 1942. The US State Department, initially refusing to believe the horrific news, investigated the reports and verified them, releasing them to the American public.

Twelve Allied governments, including the United States, Great Britain, and the Soviet Union, released the "Declaration on Atrocities" in December of 1942, condemning the 'bloody cruelties' and 'cold-blooded extermination' of Jews and vowed that the Allies would punish these war crimes.

Tricia Cundiff

18

Texas

Charles looked over at his wife. They had only switched places a few miles back; Louise had been driving while he slept. Both had enjoyed being with their families for a few days, but he had to report back to base soon. They should get into Amarillo within a couple of hours. They had driven a full day to reach Oklahoma from home, occasionally stopping to rest. Route 66 was the most direct point between Oklahoma City and Amarillo, and the views had changed from mountainous to mostly flat, with the occasional canyon spotted in the distance. The sun was hot, beating down on the windshield.

"Can't you sleep?" he asked Louise.

"No, I told you, I could drive some more. I'm too anxious to get there." Louise fanned herself with an old church fan she found under the seat. The windows down didn't help much with the heat. Tendrils of hair stuck to her neck from perspiration. Still, she looked over at her husband and smiled.

"What are you thinking about?" Charles asked, wanting conversation. The radio had so much static it was impossible to hear anything.

"I'm not sure you really want to know," Louise replied.

"I always want to know. You don't always need to tell me, but I always want to know," Charles said, half-joking.

Louise shrugged. "Okay, you asked for it. I'm thinking about the war. About everything. It's so messed up, Chaz. Somebody says one thing, like my brother, and my daddy says something else. You know, the Jews and everything. You hear everybody talking about it all the time. That's all anybody has to talk about, I guess."

"It's on everyone's mind, sweetheart. I know what you mean. We all need to escape it for a bit; the problem is that we can't. It's always right there. What do you mean about your brother and your father? Do they disagree about the war? About whether we should be in it?" Charles was confused. He had never felt any animosity about the war from her family.

"No, no. Both of them agree that we have to be there, as almost everybody does around us. You know, our neighbors. We have to do something. We can't let the Japs and the Germans take over. It's the other stuff. We keep hearing about the horrible things happening to the Jews there. It's horrible. Daddy doesn't want to believe it. He says it's the same as the last war. He said that there were lots of things about the Germans back then that weren't true, and it came out in the end. He says there's no proof. Jack says the opposite; there is proof, and we're not doing enough to stop it. I think Daddy just doesn't want to believe that people can do that to someone else; there can't be people that bad. Maybe it's his age; I don't know." Louise sighed.

"I don't want to say it, but I think it's true. There's too much for it to be made up. I guess Roosevelt's trying to do the best he can. Even if I don't like the man – you know I'm going to vote against him – he did make that refugee board for the Jews. Maybe that'll help. We keep getting reports about what's going on over there." Charles stared out the window, realizing that the war could go on much longer than he feared. People that hate other people are hard to stop.

"I guess it's different when you are fighting over a way of life or land or power. But when you're fighting because you hate another set of people, I don't know how you can win that," Louise said, echoing Charles' thoughts.

"America has to be for all people, not just people like us or look like us. That has to be what God wants, don't you think?" Charles looked over at his wife, loving that she took God's word seriously. It was gratifying to talk to someone about his faith; he felt so lucky that he had found Louise and that she was that someone.

"Of course. But then again, look what we're doing right here. We don't talk about it, but is it right?" Louise asked.

"What?" Charles glanced over at Louise, not sure what she was talking about.

"No, not the Jews. The Japanese. You know we're putting them in prison camps, right?" Louise said quietly.

"Not prison camps, detainment camps. We have to, Louise. It's for our safety, and maybe theirs, too. We don't know who's on our side or who is on the side for the Japs," Charles said as he placed his hand over hers.

"Some of them were born here! What's different about taking them from their homes and putting them somewhere they don't want to be and what the Germans are doing to Jews?" Louise shook her head.

"Well, the main thing is that we're not hurting them, Louise. We're protecting ourselves, not trying to eradicate them. Besides, I don't know how much longer we will detain them. I heard that some of them want to join our army. After all, they came here for a reason. If that reason is to live in America like the rest of us, okay then. If it's to hurt us, then we have a problem with what to do with them. But we're not monsters, Louise, unlike the Germans," Charles said. He understood his wife's concern; his own mirrored hers, but he tried to remain true to what he believed in his heart.

"Look, enough of this war talk." Charles squeezed her hand and then pointed ahead. "We'll pray about it, okay? I don't know what else we can do about this right now. But look ahead. That's Amarillo. We're almost there. Help me look for road signs."

September 11, 1944
Monday

Dear Mother, Dad & Joe,

Well, here I am in Texas. We got here last night about 5:00. We didn't have any trouble at all (Not even a flat tire). Mother, I haven't reported to base yet so I will write you as soon as I get settled and find out my new address. It sure is pretty out here. It gets pretty chilly at night but it is real nice in the day.

Louise has a bad cold but I think she has just about got it broke up now. It took us all morning to get all of Louise's clothes out and put away. We have our room all fixed up and it looks pretty nice. I think we will like it here just fine. I guess Louise will try and get a job in a few days.

Love, Charles

Love, Charles

September 19, 1944

Tuesday

Dear Mother, Dad & Joe,

I have finally got settled but I haven't started to school yet. I guess I will start some time this week. I like this post just fine. This GI Army is 10 times easier than cadets. However, when I start to school I guess it will be a little harder. I have been catching KP every other day but it isn't very hard. I get out every night until 11:30 and I think I can start getting out all night before long.

Louise had to take a civil service exam before she can get a job around here. Every job they have is a civil service job. She passed the exam easy, so I guess she will go to work in a few days. We like the place we live just fine.

Mother, I really did enjoy my visit home. I sure will be glad when this old war is over so I can come home and stay longer. I guess Dalcomb is about ready to finish up his school now. But it will take him about 3 months to take gunnery and be ready to fly. It also takes him 3 months of flying before he can go across, so he will be good for 6 months at the least.

Love, Charles

September 22, 1944

Dear Mother, Dad & Joe,

Well, I started to school, today and I like it just fine. I believe this is going to be a pretty interesting course.

Louise went to work Tuesday and she went to work for the Food Administration Board. It is a civil service job and pays

$135.00 per month. It is real close to where we live so she walks to work. It is also a real nice office and she likes it fine. I have been getting out every night and going home until 11:30. That sure is nice compared with what I was getting off.

Love, Charles

September 29, 1944

Dear Mother, Dad and Joe

I have been pretty busy lately. I go to school 6 hours a day and we have military training, PT and aircraft recognition the rest of the day. I come home every night and boy, I really do like that.

I am sure learning a lot about airplanes. We have to take them all apart and put them back.

Well, Mother, Louise is still working everyday and she likes her job all right. She hasn't been paid yet. The government only pays once a month and I think she is a little anxious to get a paycheck. We could use it, too.

How is Joe doing with his football playing this year? I guess he sure had a sore throat. I know just how sore your throat is when you have your tonsils taken out. I sure hope it helps him and I believe it will.

Dad, the war is looking better but it is sure going to push us to whip Germany by November 25.

Write when you can and take care of yourselves.

Love, Charles

19

Texas

Charles knocked lightly on the office door. He had called Louise earlier and told her he was walking down to join her. She had told him that she had to work late tonight, and he had responded by saying he would stay on base and write some letters home in the barracks. But now he had news to share, and it couldn't wait.

Louise unlocked and opened the door to the small office. "Chaz? I thought you were going to stay on base. I've still got several things to do before I can leave. It will probably be time for you to be in the barracks before I finish."

Charles reached out and pulled her to him. Hugging her, he whispered in her ear. "Is anyone else here?"

"No, I sent Sally home just a few minutes ago. She's got two kids. I told her I would take care of the rest. Everyone else has gone; that's why I have the door locked," Louise said, leaning back and looking at Charles. "Why? Whatever did you have in mind, Mr. Poag?" she said, laughing.

"Well, sure, that. But we can wait until we get home. I got this," Charles said, waving a piece of paper.

"What is it?" Louise said, reaching for it and Charles pulling it away. Grinning, he handed it to her.

Quickly reading through the paper she held, she looked up at Charles and said, "Is this what I think it is?"

"You bet. Yep, I'm staying at home tonight with my bride, with my sweetheart. It's my pass! I can live at home! With you, wherever that is." Charles picked her up and spun her around. "We're going to live like we're supposed to! Husband and wife living in the same place. I don't care where it is as long as you're there with me."

"Oh, Chaz, I'm so glad. It's so lonely when you leave at night, and then I think about you leaving and going over there to that terrible war, and I need you beside me even more," Louise said, holding on to Charles after he had set her head to spinning.

"Well, now I'll be there. And we'll worry about the war when and if that happens. We're winning, you know? We'll lick those Germans, and then we'll take care of the Japs. It'll be over soon. Ah, let's don't talk about that," he said, bending down to kiss her.

Breaking off the long kiss and breathless, Louise pushed Charles into a chair. "We can't talk about anything. And we can't do anything, either. I have work to do right now. You can go home and wait on me. I'll be there as soon as I can. Have you eaten? I've got part of a ham sandwich left from lunch?"

"Not hungry. I'm going to sit right here and write letters home. I've got lots to tell them, you know, about how my wife is so smart and got a promotion and makes all this money. My mother doesn't know you're the secretary to the big shot around here. I need to brag about my sweetheart. Working all the time, getting all that overtime, my Hot Rock is so busy making money that she has little time for her soldier," Charles said, drawing a raised eyebrow from Louise.

"Yes, be sure and tell your mother I don't have time for you. That will go over very well, I'm sure. If she only knew," Louise began.

"If she only knew what?" Charles asked. "I can tell her, you know, if you want me to pass along anything," he said, only half-joking.

"You tell your mother that your wife told you that you are the center of her world. Because you are, you know. Sure, I do like my job. It gives me something to do while waiting to be with you. You know how that guy on the radio is always talking about our primary objective?"

Charles didn't know where Louise was headed with this part of the conversation. "Sure. Our primary objective is to win each battle as it comes so that at the end of it, we can win the war."

"My primary objective is to be with you. That's it. Just to be with you. Because then I can breathe normally again."

Charles looked at Louise and slowly nodded. He understood her completely.

Their eyes met, and they smiled, so in tune with one another that they realized another milestone had been met and passed. Hearts were joined, and goals were the same. Wherever the other might be, the goal was to be together again. Forever.

Tricia Cundiff

World War II

The battles of World War II were going well for the United States and its Allies, and President Roosevelt remained popular despite his long tenure. Roosevelt had become the first president to win a third term with his victory in 1940, and there was little doubt that he would seek a fourth term. Leaders of the Democratic convention were unhappy with Roosevelt's vice-president, Henry Wallace, considering him to be set against many principles of the party. Finally, convincing Roosevelt to change his choice of a vice-presidential running mate, the convention chose Harry S. Truman of Missouri.

Governor Dewey of New York emerged as the front-runner for the Republican nomination, but few news reports gave him any chance of winning the election.

The three major world leaders – Roosevelt, Churchill, and Stalin - had mutual respect for one another. Their combined desire to drive back the German and Japanese armies brought a sort of camaraderie to the interactions. While there was a low level of trust, the working relationship was necessary to establish a unified effort to defeat the Axis powers.

Roosevelt didn't trust Churchill because he didn't like empires, and Great Britain was the greatest empire the world had ever seen. Churchill didn't trust Roosevelt because he knew that Roosevelt had a political situation at home where many people opposed American involvement in the war.

Roosevelt and Churchill distrusted Stalin, and Stalin, famously paranoid, didn't trust anyone. Roosevelt found himself in the middle, dealing with Churchill's fears of a communist takeover of Europe and Stalin's aspiration for entry into the upper realms of political and economic power.

The American people heard mixed messages on their radio reports of the actions of Churchill and Stalin; the media's intent on protecting the public's patriotism was a contributing factor in inclusion decisions.

October 19, 1944

Dear Mother, Dad & Joe,

I guess you think I am pretty slow about writing lately. They keep me pretty busy. I started on a new shift and I have to go to school from 6:00 a.m. until 12:00, then we have P.T. and military training until 4:00 p.m. than I leave to go to town at 5:00 p.m. I have to get up at 4:00 a.m. every morning so I can make it back to the base and eat chow before school time. I really like living with Louise, even if I do have to go to bed by 8:30 so I can get up at 4:00 a.m.

Mother, I sure wish I could be home and buy a horse from Uncle Jonathan. I bet he has some pretty nice horses.

Dad, I sent my vote in for Dewey today. He will at least get one vote in Tennessee. I believe Dewey has a pretty good chance to win the election. But it sure is going to be close. I voted this time for the first time and I voted for Dewey.

I had a letter from Dalcomb this week. He said he would finish in about 2 weeks. However, he has a lot of training before he would even be ready to go across. I don't even think he will ever get a chance to ever do any fighting.

Louise is working everyday. I think she likes her work fine. I sure will be glad when this old war is over so I can work and make the living for a while.

Mother, I want you to be sure and tell me what to get all of you for Christmas. Tell me at least what you would like to have and what Dad and Joe needs.

Mother, tell Joe I really liked his picture. Boy, he sure is big. He looks lots bigger than me in that picture. He isn't bad looking either. I guess he is a ladies man now. I sure hope this war is over before he gets old enough to have to go, He would be in class 1AAA.

Mother, you asked if we ever go to church. We go every Sunday; I think we have only missed about 2 Sundays since we have been here.

Love, Charles

20

Texas

Louise leaned over toward Charles, sitting at the small table in the room while they wrote letters home.

"You're doing better than me. I feel like I keep saying the same things over and over," Louise said, glancing at the letter Charles was completing.

"I seem to spend a lot of time trying to reassure Mother that Dalcomb and I will be okay. I don't think it does much good. It seems that telling her about all the men that have been over there multiple times and came back just fine hasn't helped much," Charles said as he picked up the last letter he had received from his mother. "I did tell Mother about Christmas and what we have already bought; you know, the rompers for Michael. I told her not to get me anything, but she will anyway. I told her maybe socks or underwear?" Charles looked at Louise and shrugged.

"Maybe. It's your birthday coming up, too, you know. What do you want? Give me some kind of a hint, Chaz, please?" Louise ran her fingers through his short hair.

Charles reached up and grabbed her hand. "I've got all I want right here," he said, pulling her hand to his mouth, kissing it lightly.

"Me, you've already got. Something that you really would like to have? Of course, you have to be reasonable. I can't afford a new car unless it's a really tiny one, you know, like this big," Louise said, holding her fingers a few inches apart.

"Nah, I don't need a new car. A small plane, maybe," he said, laughing.

Slapping at him playfully, Louise nodded. "Okay, let me check my bank account," she said.

"Hey, let's skip the birthday present this year. I got my present early. You are all I need, sweetheart. We've got to buy Christmas presents for the family; we can wait until next year. It's tight now, I know. You're working all the time. Let's don't spend it all. We'll save what we can and wait. I love you, my Hot Rock. No presents, okay? We'll take a day and go out riding around; maybe save some gas coupons up for a trip to the canyon and look around. Okay?" Charles had tried to figure out what to give Louise and hadn't come up with any ideas.

"No plane? Okay, maybe next year," Louise replied, returning to her letter home. "I've got to finish this. Are you going to post them on the way to base tomorrow?"

"Sure. I'll probably have more mail to bring home. One of us gets something most days," Charles said, sealing the letter's envelope to his mother. "I'll need to write Sarah, too. Maybe tomorrow."

"I worry about your sister. My sister Judy worries about how her husband is doing over there all the time, but there's no baby to think about. A new baby, and Mike isn't sure if he will be drafted. I know Sarah and Mike think about it all the time," Louise said.

"Yeah, well, Sarah can always go back home with Mother. I'm not sure Mike will do very well in the service. It's tough. He wants to get this land down there close to home. I don't blame him, but there's a lot to think about," Charles acknowledged. He stood and bent over Louise, kissing the top of her head. "I've got to get to bed. I'm beat, and you know, four o-clock comes early," he said, yawning. "You coming soon?"

"I'll be right there, Chaz; just let me finish this letter. I'll put it with yours here on the table. I need to go to the post office tomorrow anyway to mail the week's reports off. I left them on my desk at work. I'll post these at the same time," Louise said.

"You're perfect; you know that?" Charles replied, running his finger down the nape of her neck.

"Because I know the way to the post office?" Louise laughed.

"No, just because I look at you and can't figure out how someone so perfect agreed to be with me. I could just sit and look at you all night."

"Yes, in between the snoring. No, no, I'm kidding," Louise said as Charles grimaced.

"But I'm keeping you awake? You have to work, Louise; you need to sleep, too."

"I sleep enough. I don't think I could sleep as well without you here beside me. It's quite rhythmic, actually." Louise grinned. "Kind of like a lullaby."

"I'm sure that's true," Charles said, laughing.

November 11, 1944

Dear Mother, Dad & Joe,

I received your letter today. I sure hate to hear that Mike is going to have to go to the Army. I guess it will be nice to have Sarah home but I bet she had rather be with Mike. I hope they get their land all paid before he has to leave.

Mother, I had a letter from Dalcomb and he was on his way to Yuma, Arizona. I guess it will be nice in Arizona this winter but that is a small town and Dalk will probably get pretty lonesome. I sure hope he doesn't have to go across, but if he does I don't think we should worry. I think God will take care of us.

Well, Dad, I don't guess our vote did much good. However, I believe Roosevelt will do about as well as Dewey could have done by starting right in the middle of the war. I don't think it will be hard to beat him in 1948. He will probably be in such a mess that the Democrats will have a hard time ever electing another president.

I hate to hear about Bobby Ytzen having to go over. I feel sorry for his wife also. I hope I don't have any children until this war is over. I sure am glad Jimmy Swann is still alive. Being a prisoner isn't half as bad as being dead. I sure will be glad when this war is over. However, I have learned more since I have been in the Army than I ever did before.

Mother, don't worry about Dalk. It will take him about five more months before he will even be ready to go across.

Well, that's about all I know. Tell Joe to stay in there with that football and get tough. Has he made second team yet? Also tell him to stay out of that merchant marines and try to get in as a cadet. Maybe he can make it, neither of his brothers could.

Love, Charles

"I'm almost ready, Chaz. Have you got the list?"

Charles grinned, waving the paper in his hands. "Yes, sweetie, I do. I haven't laid it down since the last time you asked me." They had a couple of hours before meeting friends for supper, and this might be the last chance to do the last-minute Christmas shopping that needed to be done.

Holding her coat as she pulled up her hair, he patted her shoulder as Louise pulled a scarf tight around her neck. "It's not that cold outside, Louise. It's not far to the store, you know."

"I know. I just want to finish this up. We need to get everything mailed Monday. We've already received so many boxes from home; I feel bad that no one has ours yet. Did you warm up the car?"

"I did. So, let's go. It should be good by now. Come on, my Christmas elf, let's join the rest of the people doing their Christmas shopping. Maybe get a little Christmas spirit going?" Charles opened the door, the wind immediately pelting them with icy cold pellets.

"Oh, my, it is cold," Louise said, huddling down into the collar of her coat. They both hurried to the car.

"I don't think this is normal," Charles replied. "Tony, down at the gas station, said it's usually a lot warmer here. Not so much snow and ice as we're having."

"Okay, so this is what we have left." Charles handed the list to Louise as he pulled the car onto the road.

"There's not so much. We'll get the jacket for your dad; there's a picture frame I want to get for Judy, and then we probably need to pick up a little something to take over to Bill and Amy's. You know, since they're having us over for supper tonight." Louise placed the list in her coat pocket.

"What will we take them? I didn't know we were supposed to bring anything. Bill just said to come and have dinner with them; maybe we would play some cards or go to a movie later." Charles glanced over at Louise.

Louise shook her head. "I don't know. Maybe a little ornament for their Christmas tree? I saw some the last time we were shopping. I think they were pretty cheap, maybe one dollar? I saw one for sixty cents; it was pretty with ribbons and beads."

"Whatever you think. I hope we stay in and play cards. I was planning on going to a movie for our anniversary, you know, saving up for that." Charles reached over for her hand, slowing the car for a turn into the store's parking lot.

"Our anniversary? Oh no, I didn't forget, did I?" Louise grimaced. "No, I didn't. It's on my calendar at work. Six months. We're old married people now, aren't we?"

"Not yet. In about sixty years, we'll be old married people. And I'll be even more in love with you then, if that's possible. Will you still love me then, Hot Rock?" Charles asked, turning the car off and waiting for her reply.

"Of course, I will love you then and forever. Now, you will have to share me with Clark, you know. Just in case he drops by," Louise said, reaching over to kiss him.

"Are we talking Clark Kent? If he drops by, will he fly in?" Charles laughed as Louise poked him in the ribs.

"Sure, Clark Kent. You love those comic books, don't you? No, silly. Mr. Gable to you, Chaz. Clark to me," Louise said, laughing as she got out of the car. "Oh, my goodness, let's get inside. It's freezing out here."

Shopping didn't take very long; thankfully, the presents they had decided on were still there. Charles placed the presents in the trunk, handed the small package with the ornament for their hosts to Louise, and climbed back into the car.

"You're sure you don't want to send Mike anything?" Louise asked.

"No, I don't know where he'll be. Sarah will probably go back home and stay with Mother and Dad. The Merchant Marines will keep him away from home a lot. But I guess making six hundred dollars a month is worth it. They can save some money," Charles answered.

"Do you think that's better? I thought you said before that you didn't want Joe to go into the Merchant Marines?" Louise looked over at her husband. He didn't sound convinced that Mike had made the right choice.

"I guess it's better than going in the Army as a buck private. Maybe it's the best for him; I don't know. You know Dalcomb and me, we planned on something that we wanted to do and washed out. Preparing to do something and then doing something else, well, you never know. You have to take it as it comes and make the best of it. We're doing okay, right?"

Louise smiled. "We're doing wonderful, Chaz. Mr. and Mrs. Charles Poag are the happiest people in the whole world. We've got each other; we're together. So many are not with the people they love," she said. "It makes me sad for those that can't hold onto the ones they love."

"Yes, you're right. We are very lucky," he said, wishing he could stop the car and pull her close. The war interfered with everything, he thought. It was difficult to enjoy your happiness when you thought about the many that couldn't hold on to happiness because of the separation of war. Would he want people to feel guilty about being happy if he was over there fighting? No, of course not. But it was impossible to put aside the thoughts of battles being fought across the oceans.

"Come on, sweetheart," Charles said as they arrived at their friend's home. "Let's enjoy the evening. Bill has been on six missions in Europe, and we can celebrate that he is home with his wife. Amy is so happy to have him home, and it's nice that they invited us over. Let's concentrate on that."

Louise nodded. "You're right, Chaz. I just can't help it. I'm so happy, and then I feel guilty for being so happy," echoing, once again, Charles' thoughts.

November, 1944

Dear Mother, Dad & Joe,

We sure are having some winter weather here tonight. It started snowing this morning and has continued all day. I guess the snow is about 4 inches deep now.

I really do enjoy getting the Columbia Herald so I can keep up with what is happening in Columbia. I read where you had some snow in Columbia.

Tricia Cundiff

Mother, I am going to finish this course here in a few weeks. But they are just going to send us to another school right here on this base so I guess I will be here until about March of next year.

I think Louise is going to send your Xmas presents this week and we are just sending Sarah's there, too. Mother, I know we will like your box. You always do pretty good even if things are hard to get. Please don't open any of your presents until Xmas if you get our box before then.

Well, Louise and I celebrated our 6 month anniversary. It sure doesn't seem like I have been married for one half year, but I guess I have. I sure think I got a sweet girl. I think she is as good as they come. I hope I will be as happy the next 60 years as I have been the last 6 months.

I hate to hear about Joe being in love. He is just too young to get married (haha). I think he should wait at least another month or two until he is old enough to wear long pants.

Love, Charles

21

Texas

December 17, 1944
Sunday

Dear Mother, Dad & Joe,

I guess you think I have just quit writing. I changed shifts again this week and it takes me just about one week to get caught up.

Mother, we received your box last week and boy, it sure was nice. We opened the box of food but Louise didn't open the present. I also received my card and thanks a lot for the money. That fruit cake sure is good and Louise thought that was the best candy she ever ate. I sure liked it, too.

I guess we will have a pretty quiet Xmas. I only have Xmas day off so I think we will have Xmas dinner with a couple who we know here. I sure wish we could be home with you.

Mother, we have been to church twice today. We went to church this morning; then we went to a Xmas pageant tonight. We also went horse-back riding this afternoon. It was pretty here today, the first pretty day we have had since the snow.

I hope you all have a very happy Xmas. And I pray to God that we can all be together next Xmas.

Love, Charles

Love, Charles

World War II

The 'Christmas Truce' of 1914 achieved legendary status in history books, wherein opposing forces laid down their weapons on the battlefield and sang Christmas carols, sharing provisions. Christmas of 1944 offered little opportunity for such an event, as American troops were rarely in close contact with German forces. The Germans also began their largest counter strategy resulting in the Battle of the Bulge and heavy fighting throughout the holiday season.

There are, however, events that were heralded later as acts of peace among the fighting soldiers. Fritz Vincken was a 12-year-old in Germany who lived with his mother in an isolated cottage in the forest. He recounted the events of Christmas Eve, 1944.

American soldiers found their way through the forest and knocked on the cottage door. Fritz's mother opened the door to find two soldiers holding up a third who had been badly wounded. Communication was difficult, but they could use limited French, and Fritz's mother invited the Americans inside and attempted to make them comfortable.

Fritz recounted the evening:

"We learned that the stocky, dark-haired fellow was Jim; his friend, tall and slender, was Robin. Harry, the wounded one, was now sleeping on my bed, his face as white as the snow outside. They'd lost their battalion and had wandered in the forest for three days, looking for the Americans, and hiding from the Germans. They hadn't shaved, but still, without their heavy coats, they looked merely like big boys. And that was the way Mother began to treat them."

Fritz's mother began cooking for the soldiers when a second knock came at the door.

"Expecting to find more lost Americans, I opened the door without hesitation. There stood four soldiers, wearing uniforms quite familiar to me after five years of war. They were Wehrmacht – Germans! I was paralyzed with fear. Although still a child, I knew the harsh law: sheltering enemy soldiers constituted high treason. We could all be shot!"

The corporal leading the German patrol told Fritz's mother, "we have lost our regiment and would like to wait for daylight…can we rest here?"

"Of course," she replied, "you can also have a fine, warm meal and eat 'til the pot is empty. But, we have three other guests, whom you may not consider friends. This is Christmas Eve, and there will be no shooting here."

The corporal demanded, "Who is inside? Amerikaner?"

Fritz's mother replied, "Listen. You could be my sons, and so could they in there. A boy with a gunshot wound, fighting for his life, and his two friends, lost like you and just as hungry and exhausted as you are. This one night, this Christmas night, let us forget about killing."

Fritz said that the Americans and the Germans turned over their weapons to his mother, and she stacked them by the door, inviting them all to sit together at the table to eat. The mixed group was nervous but sat down before the lovingly cooked meal.

Fritz continued his account:

"Relaxation was now beginning to replace suspicion. Even to me, all the soldiers looked very young as we sat there together. Heinz and Willi, both from Cologne, were 16. Their German corporal, at 23, was the oldest of them all. From his food bag he drew out a bottle of red wine, and Heinz managed to find a loaf of rye bread. Mother cut that in small pieces to be served with the dinner; half the wine, however, she put away, 'for the wounded boy.' Then Mother said grace. I noticed that there were tears in her eyes as she said the old, familiar words, 'Komm, Herr Jesus. Be our guest.' And as I looked around the table, I saw tears, too, in the eyes of the battle-weary soldiers, boys again, some from America, some from Germany, all far from home. Just before midnight, Mother went to the doorstep and asked us to join her to look up at the Star of Bethlehem. We all stood beside her except Harry, who was sleeping. For all of us during the moment of silence, looking at the brightest star in the heavens, the war was a distant, almost-forgotten thing."

Fritz's recollection concluded that the truce held through the next morning when the soldiers departed after shaking hands with one another, leaving to join their respective armies.

News from the media during Christmas of 1944 included the disappearance of Glenn Miller. As Miller's musical career had soared, he had patriotically traded in his commercial success for a military uniform to entertain US troops. He took off from England on December 15, 1944, heading for France. His plane vanished over the English Channel. The band leader, a favorite during the war-weary years, was never found. The news broke on Christmas day. There have been multiple conspiracy theories about the disappearance of Miller, all unsubstantiated and most disproven. Among them are that he was assassinated after he was sent, by Eisenhower, on a secret mission to broker a peace deal with Nazi Germany. Another theory asserted that he died of a heart attack in a brothel after arriving in Paris; another advocated that his aircraft was hit by bombs being jettisoned by allied bombers returning from an aborted mission to Germany. The most likely scenario was that Miller's C-64 Norseman flew into cold weather and experienced carburetor icing (a common occurrence with the plane). This caused the aircraft to lose power and crash in the cold water. Any survivors would have quickly died of hypothermia.

Texas

December 25, 1944

Charles picked up a tendril of Louise's hair and twisted it around his finger, then tracing a line around her mouth with it. "Hey, sleepyhead, it's Christmas. Your husband is anxious to see what is in his stocking."

Louise smiled while her eyes remained closed. "We opened our presents last night, silly. It's just Christmas stockings, nothing fancy, I promise."

"I don't care. It's Christmas and it looks like Santa brought me something!" Charles tickled Louise under her chin.

Giggling, she sat up. "You're just a big kid, aren't you? Okay, okay," she exclaimed as Charles continued to tickle her. Grabbing the stockings from the table next to the bed, she handed one to Charles and put the other in her lap. "Come on, sit up, Santa's little boy, and unload your stocking."

Charles and Louise sat cross-legged on the bed, Louise watching her husband as he pulled everything from his stocking.

Apples, oranges and a small bag of nuts were in his lap. Charles looked up at Louise, confusion written across his face.

Louise sighed and laughed. "I knew you probably wouldn't get it, but I wanted you to remember. I wanted us to remember. Last Christmas, you know? You were up in Minnesota, so very far away. Christmas was hard on all of us, being apart like that. You told me they gave you some apples, oranges and nuts for Christmas. It must have made an impression on you, and I know that getting anything, especially fruit, was not easy for those nuns to put together. I want us to remember that first Christmas you were away from home, away from everyone, and how something simple made Christmas memorable. We need to remember what Christmas is about, don't we? About the birth, about Jesus, about important things like apples, oranges and nuts. Things given in the spirit of hope and love." Louise looked up at him, eyes shining.

Charles felt warmth run up his back and into his eyes, bringing tears. This woman, his wife, was truly a gift. "I don't think I'll ever look at a stocking the same way again. I don't know what to say; I had all but forgotten last Christmas since I've been so lucky to have you here this Christmas. Thank you, my dear wife, for reminding me what we should be celebrating."

"So, it was a good idea?" Louise asked, as he took her in his arms.

"The best. One that we will continue. Our first tradition, I think. Stockings with apples, oranges and nuts, every year. Not a surprise, but a reminder. Never forget to be thankful."

"Not a chance," Louise answered.

Pulling back and looking at his wife, Charles asked, "You are feeling better? I know it's been a rough week, poor thing. I'm glad the flu missed me, but so sorry you had to get it. Are you sure you feel up to going to Bill and Amy's for dinner?"

"I feel great," Louise said, taking a bite out of one of her apples. "I'm helping cook, remember?"

December 31, 1944

Dear Mother, Dad & Joe,

Here it is almost New Years, and Christmas already over again. Mother, we sure do thank you for your Christmas presents. They sure were nice and it was just what Louise and I needed. Louise really liked her sweater. We also received presents from Louise's folks. So, I guess we had a big Christmas.

We ate Christmas dinner with some friends of ours and Louise helped cook. We had chicken, cranberries, potatoes, beans, etc. It was a real nice dinner. We then went to a movie Christmas night.

Mother, I had a letter from Dalcomb and I think he is going to try to come by to see me. I sure hope he does. I really would like to see him.

Louise was sick all week before Christmas. She had a pretty bad case of the flu. She sure was sick for a few days but she is just fine now and back to work.

Dad, this war news is a little better now. I believe this last breakthrough by the Germans was just a trap by us. I believe we will get a lot of Germans before they can get back home now.

Write when you can. I want you and Dad to make a New Year's resolution not to worry about Dalcomb and I in the coming year. When the time comes for us to worry, we will all worry together.

Love, Charles

1945

22

Texas

Louise handed him the envelope as he finished his letter to his mother. "Just put it next to mine before you leave. I'll post them all tomorrow."

"Thanks, sweetheart. I've got to do better; I haven't written but one other time since Christmas. I think Dalk is as bad as I am; there's only so much we can say, and I feel like I'm repeating the same thing. Dalk said that Mother fusses at him, too, for not writing more often."

"Your mother wants to hear from you; it doesn't matter what you say, Chaz. I'm sure we'll be the same when we have kids. I think you worry anyway; it doesn't matter where you are. Of course, this war makes it worse. It's one thing to worry about your kids being happy and healthy; it's another to worry about whether they're alive or in a filthy prisoner camp. I don't know how these people stand it, month after month, sometimes years!" Louise shook her head.

Charles stood and placed the envelopes on the small table next to the door. Two other letters were ready to go with his. Turning to his wife, he pulled her close. "Stop it. Don't worry about me until there's something to worry about. Dalcomb is more likely to go across than I am, and I'm worried about him. I'm glad I got to see him, and he can go home and see Mother and Dad. It sure was good to talk to him, face to face, I mean."

"Yeah? You had a good talk, then?" Louise pulled Charles down to the side of the bed, sitting and snuggling into his arms.

"Yeah, we did. It's been a while. It's just not the same as writing letters, you know? You want to look into somebody's eyes when you're talking to them," Charles said as he looked down at Louise, smiling. "Like I'm looking at you and knowing what you're thinking."

"Oh no, you don't," she said playfully, snuggling in tighter. "Tell me about Dalcomb. Is he scared?"

"I don't think so, not any more than any of us are," Charles replied. "He seems to be more intense than he was before. I guess we all are. He said he was going to join the church while he was home. That's good. And he's going to talk to Joe about the Merchant Marines, too. Joe has to make up his own mind, but Dalk and I both think the Merchant Marines is probably his best choice."

Louise sighed. As Charles hugged her tight against him, she whispered, "I'm scared every time you leave me, just a little bit. I'll be so glad when you can come home to me every day, and we don't have to think about where you're going to be next."

"I know, sweetheart. I hate to put you through this, and maybe we should have waited to get married until I was finished, but," Charles started.

"Don't say that," Louise interrupted him. "I couldn't stand to wait another minute. I'm with you, wherever you are, you know? Oh, yes, I know there are some places I can't go, but I'm going to be here every day, praying and waiting for you, no matter where you are. This is awful, you know? And I feel guilty for feeling the way I do. There are lots of wives and mothers and fathers out there that don't know anything. Where their soldier might be, if he's okay or not. And here I am, holding you next to me, worried about you leaving," Louise shook her head, a tear falling out of the corner of her eye.

Charles touched the tear, kissing the top of her head. "I know, I know. And I hate to go, oh baby; I sure do hate to go. But I've got to get back to the base. I'm sorry I don't have time to help you pack that box to send home. I told Mother that you were sending it. Oh, and I told her that you like this sweater," he said, rubbing the soft material against her arm.

"It is soft, isn't it?" Louise said, looking up into the eyes she would miss again for the next week. "You told your mom about the stuff I'm sending? We want it; we don't want her to think we don't want it!"

"No, no. She won't think that. I just told her we didn't have room for all of it, and we'll be moving again. There's no sense in moving a bunch of stuff with us every time we go somewhere else."

"How much time do we have, do you think? Before we move again."

Charles shrugged. "I'll be through around the 15th of February; I'll find out then where I'm going, maybe. It's like Dalcomb. I was going to bring the letter I got from him, but I forgot. He said he thought he might be moved to Greenburg. If he does, he'll get fifteen more furlough days. I think he likes South Carolina okay now, but we never know where we'll be next. You know, Louise, he said that this base he's at now has German prisoners, and they're just out walking around camp without anybody watching them. They probably like it better on the American base as a prisoner than in their own country. Dalk said they have a few light details, but nothing hard. Nothing like we're hearing about how they treat the American prisoners of war."

Charles stood, grasping Louise's hand. "Got to go, sweetheart. I love you, Hot Rock; I love you so much," he said, pulling her to him for the long, soft kiss he could take with him.

Louise bit her lip as he pulled away, trying to keep herself from crying. She told herself she shouldn't cry in front of him; it made it harder for him to leave. And there was no choice. Smiling, she reached up and hugged his neck and gave him one more quick kiss. "Bye, you. I love you, too. Call me when you can."

Charles nodded as he pulled the door closed behind him. Louise sat on the bed, tears running down her face. "God, I know you're there. I know you're taking care of us. There's so much going on in this world you gave us. Please keep him safe, God. Please."

Taking a deep breath, Louise stood and looked around the small room. Pulling the box from the closet, she began loading it with the things they could send to Charles' mother.

Feb. 1945

Dear Mother, Dad & Joe,

I received your letter yesterday and I sure was glad to hear from you. I sure was glad Dalcomb and Joe joined the church.

Louise was glad to hear that her mother was getting along fine. She has been writing her pretty often but the letters aren't getting home.

I had a letter from Dalcomb. He said he might get moved to Greenburg and if he did he would get fifteen more days furlough. I sure hope he does. I don't believe Dalcomb will get a chance to fight the Germans. It looks like he will be too late. I sure hope so.

Love, Charles

I have been pretty busy for the past few weeks. I finished up school here but I think I will have to stay here for two more months for B29 training. I got to fly all last week in a B17. I got to fly it a little by myself. It is just like a big truck. I sure hope I get on B29s. I like them much better than a B17.

Mother, I sure want Joe to sign up with Merchant Marines before he gets 18 years old, and has to sign up for the Army. I sure hope he gets into the Merchant Marine cadets.

I will keep you informed as to how I come out on this B29 deal. But at present it looks like I will be here for another month or so.

Love, Charles

World War II

The last of January 1945 ended the Battle of the Bulge, resulting in the German army's retreat into Germany. Bombing raids began on the German city of Dresden, with thousands of civilian lives lost. Over a thousand Allied bombers peppered the ground and created a firestorm.

In the Pacific, the US Navy began bombing an island of Japan, recalled as the Battle of Iwo Jima. Three days after the bombing started, the US Marines landed on Iwo Jima and raised the US flag on Mount Suribachi several days later. While over 20,000 Japanese defenders were on the island, approximately one thousand were taken prisoner. Different theories support the reasoning for the death of so many Japanese during this battle. The Allied forces were well aware of the atrocities committed by the Japanese toward prisoners of war. They had little sympathy for their plight as the supplies and food dwindled on the island during extended days of battle. Additionally, the Japanese would more often than not fight to the death, believing that otherwise was dishonorable.

On January 27, 1945, Soviet Soldiers liberated the Auschwitz concentration camp. As the Red Army approached, the Nazis forced over 60,000 prisoners to begin a death march away from the camp, leaving behind 7000 that were too weak to walk. Word spread quickly of the horrors found at the camp, and the Allies were shocked at the evil within the walls of the Nazi prisons.

Love, Charles

News reports traveled quickly through the military portals. Soldiers in every part of the world and training bases in the United States heard of the terrible conditions of the camps. It was impossible to contain the horrific findings and prevent their reports from broadcasting to the American public, even with the mandatory censorship of mail and media reporting.

Florida

March, 1945

Dear Mother, Dad, Joe, Sarah & Michael,

Here I am in Florida. I guess Louise has been by to see you. She was coming by home before she came on down. It sure is wonderful weather down here now. It is really hot in the middle of the day, but it is cool at night. Everything is green and flowers blooming.

This is a small base and it is as many officers here as there is enlisted men. This town of Sebring is smaller than Columbia, about the size of Mt. Pleasant. The town is right on a lake and is sure a pretty little town.

I am going to work on airplanes here until gunnery school opens up again. Some of the fellows have been here for 6 or more months, but I don't know how long I will be around.

I have Louise a place to live here. It is just a room in a hotel but everybody lives in hotels here. This town is pretty crowded. We sure was glad to get out of Texas for a while. However, it does get plenty hot here. I will write more when I find out something.

Love, Charles

Charles placed the short letter in the envelope and sealed it. He could post it tomorrow. Glancing around the temporary barracks he lived in; the other men were quiet. Chow time at breakfast that morning had been boisterous and loud until one of the officers walked in with pictures that had been sent from the front lines in Europe. They had received more photos of the horrors found at the concentration camp their Soviet allies had liberated. Even the officers at the base seemed to be more restrained than usual, refraining from barking orders at the enlisted men.

Charles found himself at a loss; what do you pray for when such unimaginable acts by men are committed? How do you hold down your hate and anger at such cruelty?

There were things he couldn't share with his parents; he couldn't even begin to think about telling Louise about the pictures. Of course, the news reports were sketchy, but enough had leaked, so the American public was aware that the rumors about the Nazi atrocities were true. The rumors had circulated before the beginning of the US involvement. The Nazis had committed crimes against God himself, and confronting and destroying that evil was more important than any thoughts of retreat. Seeing the evidence of the men, women, and children that had suffered such horrible conditions and treatment was enough to silence those against the war effort. If war was the answer to the evil that existed, there must be war.

Charles missed Louise. He ached inside to hold her. Times like this did not need words, and she seemed to know that. Their hopes and dreams for the future were always held just a little bit in check because of the unknowns surrounding the war. Proud to do his duty for his country and the life he had been blessed to have, he prayed for an end to the war and for God to conquer the evil happening in Europe, and from the reports he had heard, the evil in the Pacific. Praying together, he and Louise echoed each other's thoughts. But there were times she thought he was asleep that her whisperings reached his ears. 'My Lord, I can't think of living without my Chaz. Please take care of him on the nights I can't hold him. If they take him over there, God, please, please, don't let anything happen. You sent him to me, Lord. Please let me keep him.'

It had taken all his strength not to turn over and hold her. Her private moments with God were hers; he knew how she needed that as he needed his time with God. Even when he knew he was not being fair and questioned what God was doing in this war, his mother's words and faith brought him back to the reality of God's love and our inability to see what He had in store. He thought again of the horrible pictures taken at Auschwitz. How could God let this happen?

"Charley? Hey, some of us are heading down to the lake for a swim. Come on, we can't just sit here; I can't stand it," said Bobby McKay, a Tennessee man Charles had befriended when he arrived.

"Yeah, come on, Charley-boy. We'll throw around a little football, too. We've got all day to kill," said another man in the barracks. Several men had already left the barracks, the day's heat penetrating through the windows and beckoning everyone outside in the cooler breezes.

"Sure thing," Charles replied, happy to take his thoughts elsewhere. Sometimes, he guessed, God understood that you were too angry or scared to pray. It had to be enough that he knew God was there, waiting for him to be quiet and listen to Him. Louise would not arrive at the earliest for a few more days; he was lonesome and bored.

Bobby turned back to Charles. "Oh yeah, I placed a letter on your bunk, under your pillow, so it wouldn't get lost. It was mixed up in my letters from home. I guess the guys in the mail room are getting in too big a rush to finish up."

Charles pulled the letter out from under his pillow. Staring at the return address listed as California, he tore open the envelope. "You go ahead; I'll be there in a minute. It's probably from Frank Liston, another guy that wanted to be a pilot, he didn't put his name on the top, and I haven't heard from him since I left Santa Ana."

Bobby nodded, tossing a football up in the air. "All right then, see you out there. We're down on the other end of the field at the lake."

Love, Charles

Charles looked at the bottom of the letter and was surprised to see Sonny Powell's signature there. He had been in Santa Ana but not in their barracks. He had been a member of Charles' crew for a few weeks. His eyes were drawn to Frank's name. Oh no. Charles sat down on the bed. Frank in France? How could he have gotten there that quickly? Charles didn't want to finish reading it; he knew in his heart what it said. There was no reason for Sonny Powell to contact him unless it was bad news. Frank was gone.

Charles took a deep breath. He couldn't hold back the tears, though he quickly wiped them away and looked around the barracks to see if anyone was still there. He shook his head; in times like this, when you needed privacy, it was nowhere to be found. It's not that he hadn't seen soldiers crying, but you did your best to hold it in. Women cry; men hold it in.

Memories took him back to boot camp, Minnesota, and Santa Ana. Frank washed out, too. He must have immediately opted to go with the ground troops. It's not like they would turn anyone down that wanted to go over; once you got past the tests, they needed men. Frank gone. Charles' eyes went back to the letter. They had finally located Frank's mother and would send his body to her when it arrived in the next transport. There was little else in the letter from Sonny; he had supposed that Charles would want to know.

Charles had made many friends during his time in the Army Air Corps. Frank had been his closest. He was gone. Charles ached for Louise, but it was probably best to deal with this alone. He hoped that Frank hadn't been alone when it happened.

Tricia Cundiff

23

Florida

March 15, 1945

Dear Mother, Dad, Sarah, Joe & Michael,

Well, how is everything in Columbia these days. It sure is hot down here. I have been out in the sun quite a bit and I guess I am going to be pretty blistered. I look just like a little glow worm now I am so red.

I sure like this place better than Texas. But the town here is really small and it is kindly hard to find a good place for Louise to live. However, I got her a nice room now so I feel lots better about the place.

I am working on the line here; I am a propellor (big shot) specialist at present, however I have been trying to get transferred to something else because on propellors we have to work two weeks days and two weeks nights. I am on nights now; I go to work at 5:00 in the afternoon and work until about 11:00 at night. That isn't so bad, but if Louise works here she will probably get off at 5:00 and so we won't be able to be together very much.

Louise will be here tomorrow I guess. I sure will be glad when she gets here. I sure miss her a lot.

I guess that is about all I know now. I sure wish I had been sent out to Smyrna air Base like J. T. Luster. I never could have that kind of luck.

Love, Charles

"Oh my gosh, aren't you the prettiest thing ever?" Charles said as he lifted Louise off the ground and spun her around.

Louise laughed as she hugged his neck. "You must not have much to look at around here," she said, glancing around the small courtyard next to her room. "I like the room, Mr. Poag; I think it will suit us just fine."

"You're so wrong about that, Mrs. Poag. I have plenty to look at, barracks and airfields, propellors and planes, and oh yeah, I still have that picture of Hedy Lamarr, you know." Charles laughed as he sat her down.

"The picture I gave you from that newspaper article? You stare at that every day, do you?" Louise straightened her skirt, looking up at Charles through raised eyebrows.

"She doesn't hold a candle to you, Hot Rock," Charles replied, looking around the small spaces allowed for cars. "The place is okay; I wish I could have found you something bigger."

"This is fine, Chaz. We'll just be moving again soon, anyway," Louise said, pulling him to her. "How are you, my husband?"

"I'm good. So, trouble with the car, huh? I'm glad you were close to a service station. No more problems after that, though, right?" Charles patted the top of the hood.

"No, no more trouble. That's not what I meant, Chaz. How are you doing, really? I'm so sorry about Frank. He was a good man, I'm sure. I didn't know him well, but I know it's hard on you." Louise didn't know what to say but hated that Charles had to deal with it alone.

"I'm okay, truly. I can look at it this way, Louise. He started going to church; he had not gotten married, which was a good choice for him, I think. Maybe he just needed to get away, and he thought that was the best way to do it. I don't know. I guess it's God's will. I don't understand it," Charles said, looking off into the distance. Shaking his head, he continued. "Enough of that, my beautiful wife. Let me show you around the big town of Sebring, Florida!"

"I drove here, remember, Chaz? I think I've already seen it. All two blocks of it," Louise said, grinning.

March 22, 1945

Dear Mother, Sarah, Dad, Joe & Michael,

Louise made it here just fine; a wire on the coil broke but she happened to be at a service station, so she got it fixed right there. Louise said you, Dad and Sarah all looked in better health than she had ever seen you. Maybe Michael is good to have around if you won't worry so much.

Mother, I got a 3-day pass last Sunday so Louise, Judy, and I went down to Miami and West Palm Beach. We all really enjoyed it; it was the first time Louise and Judy had ever been there so they were really thrilled.

I sure hated to hear about Winfrey Morell's husband. This old war is really bad, sometimes I don't see why God lets such things happen. But I guess it must be for the best someday. The war news sounds pretty good now. I don't believe Dalcomb, Mike or I will get to fight the Germans at all. Even the Japs news sounds good to me. I believe this will be over before long.

Mother, I have changed jobs again; I am in a different squad. But I am still on the line, I guess I will get a little flying here as student engineer. I don't know how long we will be here but I don't care if we stay for months. I like this field okay.

Sarah, thanks for your letter. Write me every time you can. I enjoy your letters. Look after old Joe. He must really be a ladies' man.

Love, Charles

"Here you go, sweetheart. I saved you three cookies. That's what I had for lunch," Charles said, handing Louise the small box he had received from his mother.

"Well, that's not enough. Why didn't you go to the dining room?" Louise asked, opening the box and taking a bite out of the cookie on top.

"I was full of cookies by then. The mess hall was full, anyway. It's pretty small here, and the officers take it over," Charles said, pulling her to him.

Reaching up to kiss him between bites, Louise said, "So what did my soldier boy do today?"

"Same thing. I drive the caterpillar around and go between putting gas in the tanks I'm pulling and putting the gas into the planes. It's pretty boring. How about you? Lonely since Judy left?"

Louise nodded. "Yes, and she only just left yesterday. But I had plenty to do; I start to work tomorrow!"

"Whoa! That was quick. So, you got the job at that ordinance depot?" Charles was surprised; she had only applied yesterday after her sister left to return home.

"Yes, sir! I start tomorrow. They called me this morning. It gives me something to do. Besides, we can use the money, Chaz."

"I know, I know. Still, I wish you could stay at home in a little house with a garden outside, taking care of our babies," Charles said, smiling down at her.

"And where would you be in this wishing world of yours?" Louise laughed.

"Why, I would be working, of course, flying airplanes around the world. But I would be home every night to play with the children, all eight of them, and then, after we put the children to bed, all eight of them, we would make love until time for me to go back to flying planes the next day," Charles said, enjoying his fantasy and grinning at his wife.

"I'm not quite sure who this wife is you're planning on coming home to after flying around the world in a very fast airplane," Louise began, giggling when Charles picked her up and swung her around.

"Why, every one of those eight children looks just like you, so it must be you!" Charles let her down and sat on the side of the bed. "Whew!"

"Not too tired, are you? Maybe we need to talk about how many children we might have. You're not serious about that, are you?" Louise questioned, not altogether kidding.

"Ah. We'll let God handle that part. You know, God and you and me. No, of course not," Charles said, seeing the look on Louise's face. "Eight might be too many."

"You think so?" Louise laughed. "Oh, Chaz. I'll be glad when we are ready to start our family."

"Me, too. When this war is over, let's see. Do I want a bunch of little Louises running around?" Charles twirled a lock of his wife's hair around his finger. "Yes, I believe I do."

Louise nodded. "What about some little Charleys? We could have a bunch of little Charleys, Dalcombs, or Joes. I remember when my little brother was small. Jack was a handful; he still is. You know why he didn't bring me all the way to California to get married, right?"

Charles paused, thinking. "It had something to do with a girl, right?"

"Charlene. His sweetheart. He had to get back to Old Hickory; he couldn't wait another few days and bring me to you." Louise shook her head.

"Well, I might have done the same thing if it meant getting back to you," Charles replied. "Love does strange things to people. Makes you forget all about other things."

Louise put her arms around him. "What kind of things?"

"Oh, let me think about a few," he said, pulling her close. Whispering in her ear, he said, "Like making me forget where I have to be in just a couple of hours. Like making me want to bury myself in your neck, smelling your perfume, kissing you like this." Charles had yearned for these moments, moments when the memories of the horrific pictures of war he had seen could be thrust to the back of his consciousness, a time for love to overcome the anger and despair of conflict. Memories of Frank and other friends lost in the war interrupted sleep and occupied his thoughts during boring, repetitive hours on base; it was a relief to push those aside and concentrate on his wife.

World War II

The first concentration camp liberated by US troops occurred on April 4, 1945. Ohrdruf concentration camp, located near Gotha in Germany, garnered the attention of General Dwight D. Eisenhower, Supreme Commander of the Allied Forces in Europe, because of the ghastly nature of the findings of the soldiers as they entered the camp. Eisenhower, along with General George Patton and General Omar Bradley, visited the camp on April 12 and reported to General George C. Marshall, the head of the Joint Chiefs of Staff in Washington, D.C. The horrors witnessed at the camp were recounted by all three, as well as the soldiers that had initially arrived. Eisenhower later requested that members of Congress and journalists be given permission to visit the camps and received immediate permission to bring the horrible truth about German Nazi atrocities to the American public.

Vice-President Harry S. Truman became the 33rd President of the United States after the unexpected death of Franklin D. Roosevelt. On the afternoon of April 12, 1945, while sitting for a portrait in his home in Warm Springs, Arkansas, Roosevelt complained of a terrible headache. Slumping forward in his chair, unconscious, he was carried into his bedroom and attended to by his physician. After a diagnosis of a massive intracerebral hemorrhage, Roosevelt died at the age of 63 at 3:35 p.m.

Florida

April 17, 1945

Dear Folks,

It sure was too bad about the President's death. I had a letter from Dalcomb yesterday and he said he was going to school. I believe they will have the Germans whipped if he don't hurry up and get over there. Our Army generals figure out our military strategy, so the President's death won't affect the war, I don't think.

Mother, tell Sarah I am sorry I hurt her feelings about Mike. I was trying to carry on a little fun with him. I was only joking. I guess the reason I like to joke with him is just because I am jealous of him. I think he is really smart. I wish I was just half as well learned on some things as he is. I won't say anything else.

Well, Dad, how is everything. I am going to send you some more cigarettes if you want them. Of course, due to my financial condition, it will cost you $1.50 per carton; they are 15 cents per pack.

I guess old Joe was really a dude in stunt night. Has he decided to get into the merchant marines when he finished school? If he doesn't they will sure draft him and put him in the infantry.

Love, Charles

Louise looked up from the letter Charles had written, her brow furrowed and a question in her eyes.

"What?" Charles asked, addressing the envelope.

"How did you hurt Sarah's feelings? Are they mad at you about something? I can't imagine Sarah being mad at anyone," Louise said, shaking her head.

"Oh, I said something in another letter about Mike being a glorified civilian in a uniform; that I didn't have to salute him or something like that. I was just kidding around, but I guess Sarah didn't see it like that. Or Mike didn't. I don't know. Anyway, I guess I used the wrong words. That's why I tried to say I'm sorry in this letter. I'm not going to say anything else about it," Charles said, shrugging. He handed her the envelope. "Mail this tomorrow for me, please?"

"Of course, I have letters to everyone to post too." Louise laid the letter beside her purse. "Have you heard anything? Where we're going next?" She looked around the tiny hotel room. "Not that I don't just love it here," she laughed.

"No, not yet. But I think we're going back to Amarillo, sweetheart. I got the B29 engineer's course. B29s are only in Amarillo and Denver. I wish we could go to Smyrna, but that's not going to happen," Charles said, shaking his head.

"When? Do you know?"

"No, but it should be in the next week or two. I know you'll be glad to get out of here, anyway. It's hard to live out of a hotel room, and we've been here a while," Charles said, pulling Louise down onto his lap.

"Texas is so hot," Louise said, snuggling into his shoulder.

"Yes, it is. Louise, you know, you don't have to go. You could go back home and wait until I get stationed somewhere I'll be for a while. I'll probably be in Amarillo for five or six months and then in Denver for a few more months. I hate for you to have to keep moving around," Charles kissed the top of her head.

"Stop it. I'm going where you go for as long as the Army will let me. Go back home? No, no, no. Home is where you are. I love my family, Chaz; I love your family. My home is always where you are; you're my home," Louise said, grabbing his shirt.

"Okay, okay. You go unless I go over." He felt Louise stiffen in his lap and quickly continued. "I love that you want to be with me, to travel around to all these base towns and wait for me to be with you. I always have something to look forward to with you around. Oh, Hot Rock, I love you so much."

"And I love you, Chaz-Bo. No matter where you are, that's where I am. Even if you're over there, my heart goes with you; my soul goes with you. I'm empty until you come back to me," Louise said, staring into his eyes.

Charles nodded, unable to answer. How he loved this woman.

April 24, 1945

Dear Mother, Dad & all,

Well, folks, I guess I will be moving again in a few days. I am going back to Amarillo, Texas for B29 engineers course. I sure was glad to be able to get on B29s but I sure hated to have to go back to Texas. This engineers course will take about 5 or 6 more months, so maybe the war will be over by then; I sure hope so anyway. Louise is going to travel with me if they will let me go by car, but if they don't I guess she will come by home again before she comes out to Texas. I am sure hoping I can travel with her from here. I can't possibly get a furlough or a delay in route but maybe I can get a furlough when I finish this B29 course.

It sure was bad about Roosevelt, but I believe Truman will be as good a democrat as we can have. We just should have Dewey.

Save those chickens, Mother. I may be home some time and I will sure help you eat them. You are really having good luck by only losing 3 chicks out of 50. I sure hope

Dad can get his garden in and raise a lot of food. I want you to save a little money now if you possibly can so you can build you a little house after this war.

Love, Charles

April 28, 1945

Dear Mother, Dad, & all,

I finished processing yesterday so I am off until I ship tomorrow. I leave Sunday at 12:00 o'clock and I guess I will be in Amarillo about Friday of next week. I will write you and send you my new address just as soon as I get there.

Louise is going to leave here either Tuesday or Wednesday, so she will probably be home Friday or Saturday. She will call you just as soon as she arrives. I sure wanted to travel with her, but I couldn't so she is going to come by home and stay about a week before she comes on out to Texas.

What has Joe decided to get in? I hope he is still interested in the Merchant Marines; I believe that is just as good as anything and lots better than the infantry. He can make lots more money also.

How is Sarah and Michael. Tell Dad and Joe to be careful. I'll write you again as soon as I get to Amarillo.

Love, Charles

Tricia Cundiff

24

World War II

There were over 400,000 American casualties in World War II, six of those occurring on the American mainland. The Japanese created fire-balloon bombs, made to float across the Pacific and explode over the western United States. Of the approximate 9000 of these balloons released by the Japanese, only 342 of them reached American soil. Most were shot down, and the rest fell on their own. Except for one that fell in rural Oregon on May 5, 1945, there were no casualties.

Reverend Archie Mitchell was driving his wife, Elyse, and the elementary Sunday School class she taught to a picnic near Klamath Falls in Oregon when his wife began to feel sick. She was pregnant then, so her husband pulled over to give her a moment. As she recovered from her momentary nausea, she and her class of children wandered into a field while her husband chatted with construction workers nearby. The construction workers and Reverend Mitchell heard a blast; Elyse and five of the school children died due to Japan's balloon campaign.

Allied forces began to discover the horrible scale of the Holocaust as they advanced into Germany, journalists reporting the accuracy of the previous information given to the American public. The war in Europe gathered quick momentum with the execution of Mussolini on April 25 and the suicide of Adolf Hitler on April 30, 1945.

German forces across Europe began surrendering their forces to the Allies. General Eisenhower threatened to break off negotiations unless the Germans agreed to a complete unconditional surrender to the Allies on all fronts.

On May 8, 1945, British Prime Minister Winston Churchill said hostilities would end one minute after midnight. The War in Europe was over.

Amarillo, Texas

"Chaz? Is it true?" Louise's voice was high, anticipation in her tone.

"Yes. You're hearing the same thing I am, sweetheart. It has to be true. There's not much celebrating going on here, but there's a difference in how people are talking now. We've still got the Japs to take care of, but Hitler's dead, and the war is over in Europe. Now we have a lot of cleaning up to do, is what I hear," Charles cradled the phone on his shoulder, thankful that he had been called into the base communication office for the phone call. They wouldn't often come and get you for a call unless it was bad news. He had hurried to the phone, imagining all kinds of horrible things happening at home before he heard Louise's voice and her question. Breathing more easily, he continued. "Hitler got scared, I guess. That woman he married killed herself, too. He should have been scared, having to answer for all the horrible things he did. Some of us wish we had been able to capture him. He deserved to suffer.

"Oh, Chaz. I'm just glad it's over. We hear good news about Japan, too. Wait, here's your mother. We just finished supper. I'm in the kitchen, and your mother wants to talk to you, too," Louise said. Charles imagined her sitting around the old table in his mother's kitchen with his parents, brother, and sister. How he wished he could be there.

"Oh my, Charles. It's so good to hear you. I'm glad we got you, you know; it just feels real when you say it. We've been listening to the radio and heard so much terrible stuff; it's so nice when you hear something good. We tried to call Dalcomb, too, when we couldn't get through to you," she said, out of breath.

"Hi, Mother. It's good to talk to you, too. Did you talk to Dalcomb?" Charles asked.

"No, we couldn't get him on the phone. I guess we were lucky to get you. Here's your dad. Oh, and Joe's here, too. He wants to say hello. I love you, Charles. You take good care of yourself, now. And write me. Maybe everybody will get to come home soon. We're praying hard about it."

Talk of nothing but the war and some kidding with Joe about his girlfriend, Louise returned to the phone. "Chaz? I love you. I'll be there soon, I promise."

Charles answered, "I know, sweetheart. I'm looking for you a place to live. Got to go; they've got a line of people in here. Love you."

Several hundred miles away in Tennessee, Louise placed the phone back in its cradle, turned to Charles' family, her family now, and smiled. "He's good; he sounds good. Didn't he?" She couldn't help it; tears fell down her face. The horrors they had heard about from the German camps preyed upon their thoughts. One enemy down, another one to go. Hopefully, this war will be over soon.

Charles' mother came and wrapped her arms around her son's wife. "Louise, it's good. You'll be seeing him soon, you know. I only wish I could go with you. It would be so good to have my boys home where they belong. All of them," she said, looking over at her youngest, Joe.

Love, Charles

May 11, 1945

Dear Mother, Dad, Sarah and all,

I received both your letters today. I was glad to hear from you and I sure was glad to get to talk to you all on Wednesday night. I had a letter from Dalcomb this week also. He told me about his training. I hope he is sent to Germany now instead of Japan. This old war is getting along nicely but it looks pretty bad for Dalcomb and I. I guess we will have to fight the Japs. But I believe they will be pretty easy to handle. I believe in the air is the safest way to fight Japs. They don't have many planes and they aren't very good.

Sarah, it looks like I am kindly behind on this starting a family. I sure would like to see Michael; he will probably be a good man if he doesn't get spoiled! Tell Mike I hope he can stay on the Mississippi this whole war. That is lots safer than the Pacific.

Joe, I got your announcement of graduation. I wish I could come and see you, but I don't guess I will be able to make it.

Tell Joe he had better be careful or they will have him in the infantry before he has a chance to get into what he wants.

Love, Charles

Charles looked around the room; he had made up the bed and placed a few of his things in the bottom drawer of the dresser. He would only be here one night a week, but it made him and Louise feel better if he had a presence in the room, even when he was on base. He was released on Saturday night and had to be back on base on Sunday night at 9:30. At least he had some time with Louise. He was anxious for her to get here. It had been almost three weeks since he had seen her.

Of course, this wouldn't be a regular reunion; Judy was coming with Louise. So it would be next weekend before they could be alone. It's okay, he told himself. Just seeing her would be enough for now.

Charles looked down at his watch. They should be getting here any time now. He glanced around the room again. The landlady for the room he had rented was a dear person. Louise would have kitchen privileges, which was good since Judy said she would teach Louise to cook while she was here. Charles grinned, shaking his head. Louise was determined to learn to cook, probably because he always bragged about his mother's cooking. He had told her often that he didn't care if she ever learned to cook, he would love her anyway, and besides, they could always eat at his mother's house. That probably helped her to decide she was going to learn to cook.

A knock at the door and Charles opened it to find the landlady, Mrs. Compton, standing there with a plate of cookies. Laughing, he told her he had been thinking about food.

Mrs. Compton handed him the plate and picked up the jar of lemonade she had placed on the floor. "Here you go. I know your wife is arriving today, right? I wanted to make her welcome. No need to spend any time with me, you know. Just the normal introductions, then you two visit," she said.

"You're so nice! Thank you so much. Louise is bringing her sister with her, remember? Judy, her sister, will be here for a few days, but they won't be a bother, I promise," Charles assured her.

"A bother? Goodness, no. It will be nice to have someone in the house; it's lonely when no one is here. And I have all this room. Two more bedrooms that are empty! Well, for now, anyway," she said, beaming.

"Yes! Have you heard any more from your son?" Charles asked.

"No, but I know he's on his way. Every day I wake up and think that this could be the day I see him again," she said, her eyes wet with happy tears. "Oh my, this old woman better get back to the kitchen. I have another batch of cookies in the oven!" Mrs. Compton wiped her eyes with a corner of her apron and turned away.

Charles closed the door softly. The landlady's story was a common one. Her son had been a prisoner of war for a year, and she had finally heard from him. He was a lieutenant, a bombardier, and his plane had been shot down. He was finally free and on his way home. Never give up, he thought to himself. There is always hope.

Voices beyond the door a few minutes later made him smile. The lilt in Louise's voice came to his ears, and he thought his heart skipped a beat. Wow, he thought. Love does all kinds of things to you.

Laughing, Charles pulled Louise into his arms when she opened the door. With Judy and Mrs. Compton looking on, he kissed her long and tenderly, enjoying the taste of her lips and the smell of her hair. "I didn't know how much I missed you until just now," he said as he reluctantly pulled back and looked down at her.

"Well, I hope it was a lot! Because I missed you more than I could even explain," Louise said as she patted his shoulders and chest to reassure herself that she was in his arms.

Convincing Mrs. Compton to stay and enjoy a cookie and lemonade with them, Judy and Louise talked with the landlady, exclaiming over her wonderful home and how nice it was that she opened it up to relatives of servicemen.

Charles had told Louise about Mrs. Compton's son, and they all listened as she told them about his disappearance and when she found out he was a prisoner of war. Louise and Judy both cried with her when she told of the joy of finding out that he was coming home. Charles sat back on the bed and watched the three of them talk, staring at his wife.

Louise glanced over at him and noticed him staring. Smiling, her eyes saying everything that needed to be said, she turned back to Mrs. Compton.

"I'll need to leave by ten to get back on base," Charles said after Mrs. Compton had hugged them all and left, closing the door softly behind her.

"So why don't I go take a walk or something?" Judy said, watching her sister and brother-in-law stare at one another.

"No, no, Judy. I didn't mean that at all," Charles said, shaking his head.

"He's right, Judy," said Louise. "You stay here. It's dark out, and while I'm sure this is a safe neighborhood," she said, looking over at Charles and smiling when he nodded, "you don't need to be out walking around this late by yourself."

"Oh, it's okay. Look, you've only a few minutes before Charles has to leave. You need a few minutes to talk alone. I can go and help Mrs. Compton clean up the kitchen, okay? I'm sure she'll be happy for me to come and help. Besides, I can look at the setup I'm going to have in order to turn you into a world-class cook, Louise. I may need a lot of help," she said, laughing as Louise raised her eyebrows.

Charles pulled Louise into his lap after Judy left to help Mrs. Compton. "Oh woman, you have me wrapped around your little finger, you know that?"

"I'm so glad to be here. It's been a long trip. Oh, I brought pictures," she said, pulling an envelope out of her purse. "Here's some of Michael. He's so cute. I'm not sure who he looks like. And this is a good one of all three of them."

"Yeah, he's a good-looking boy, isn't he?" Charles flipped through the pictures. "Sarah still looks like she's put on some pounds, though, doesn't she?"

"She's lost some since I saw her last. It takes a bit to get rid of that baby weight. Don't you dare say anything to her; she is really sensitive about it. Mike has lost a lot of weight, hasn't he?" Louise said, pointing out the picture of Mike in his uniform.

"Yes, he does look good; he looks like a big shot, huh?" Charles laid the pictures down. "What about Joe? Does he talk about what he's going to do? He'll be eighteen soon; he better decide."

"I think he's good with the Merchant Marines," Louise said, snuggling closer.

Charles tilted her head up to his. "I've got to go, but I don't want to."

"And I don't want you to, but I know you have to," Louise answered, reaching up and pulling his face to hers, taking in the smell of his breath and the warmth of his kiss.

May 27, 1945

Dear Mother, Dad & all,

I received your letter today, sure was glad to hear from you. I have finally started to school. I sure like this B29, it sure is a nice airplane and it sure is big. It has a wing longer than your house. It weighs 45 tons and has 8800 horse power. It will carry 20 tons of bombs. Ask Dad if that isn't big. It is bigger than a railroad train. They sure keep us busy around here. I have to get up at 4:15 and I am on the run until 8:00 at night. I only get out on Saturday night but Louise can come out and see me on Thursday night.

Louise has a job. She went to work today and said she thought she was going to like her job. We like her place to live just fine. Louise cooked dinner for me Sunday and she sure did surprise me. She can really cook good. The lady she lives with is helping her out. We had boiled ham, stewed potatoes, white beans, fresh corn, lettuce salad and tomatoes, tea and a dessert. I sure was proud of her, it was the first meal she ever cooked.

It sure is dry and hot out here. It doesn't rain at all, but the wind and sand blows all the time.

Has Joe decided what he is going to get into yet. Tell him I will try and send him something before long when I get a pay day.

Love, Charles

"It's lucky that our anniversary ended up on a Sunday, isn't it?" Charles said as he held his bride of one year in his arms, watching the sun peek in through the curtains at the window. He and Louise appreciated the privacy the rented room gave them, especially since they were only together for the weekend. The room was small, but it was on the upper floor of the house.

"Aw, yes, we are lucky," Louise said, enjoying the feel of his arms around her. "It's nice to wake up next to the man you've been married to for a year. It's awful lonesome every morning when you're not here. I'm good staying in all day. We're running a little short of money right now, Chaz; we don't need to spend any. I'll get paid Friday, and then it will be a little easier."

"I think we can afford that movie you've been talking about. It's showing down at the movie palace. 'Arsenic and Old Lace.' You can sit and watch that handsome Cary Grant and swoon over him. Some of my competition, huh?" Charles kissed the top of Louise's head.

"You have no competition, my handsome husband, none at all. It's supposed to be a good movie, that's all," Louise said, stretching and reaching for her robe.

Charles reached to pull her back into bed. "Let's stay here and talk awhile. It's early yet."

"Sadie probably has the coffee on. I'll grab us some and come back up," Louise said, pulling the robe around her waist and tying it. Mrs. Compton was considerate of her boarder's limited time with her husband and, after making coffee on Sunday morning, would usually leave early to go to church and prepare for the service, filling up the small cups with grape juice for communion. Louise and Charles accompanied her to church occasionally, but Mrs. Compton knew today was a special day. A first anniversary only comes once.

Louise returned a few minutes later with two steaming cups of fresh-brewed coffee. Charles had risen and opened the curtains and blinds holding out the day, making a place for them to sit and enjoy the morning sunshine with their coffee.

Savoring the smell, Charles closed his eyes as he sipped the hot liquid. "Perfect," he said. "I don't get this kind of service in the barracks."

"I would hope not. I'm supposed to be the only one bringing you anything to bed!" Louise said, laughing.

"I can assure you that is true," Charles said, laughing with her. "It will be nice, though, someday, don't you think? That we really, truly live together all the time? It seems like we're in a holding pattern, doesn't it? Waiting for the time to truly start?"

"I know what you mean. But at least we're waiting together. All the husbands over there and their wives are here praying there will come a time when they can start again. At least now, if they're in Europe, they will probably get home. But if they're in Japan," Louise began, then shook her head.

"Don't worry, sweetheart. Look at Mrs. Compton! She's been waiting a year for her son, and now, he's free. He's coming home. We never give up; that's why we're going to win. We never give up."

"Have you heard from Dalcomb?" Louise asked. "I saw the letter from Sarah," she said, motioning to the letters Charles had left on the desk, "but there's nothing from Dalcomb."

"No, I haven't heard from him in over a week. I guess he is pretty busy. I don't know if he'll get to go home again before he has to go over." Charles reached over and took one of Louise's hands. "We've been very lucky, both of us, DalK and I. Not many guys stay in the states for two years as we have. It's okay if we go, Hot Rock; it really is. We'll be in the air; that's better than on the ground. I don't think these Japs are going to last much longer." He sat back and took another sip of coffee. "Now, Joe, on the other hand, better do something soon. If he doesn't, he will get drafted into the infantry. The Army ground troops are in the middle of it all. He doesn't want that; I don't think."

"Really, Chaz, who does? I know, I know, it's your duty; it's what men do. I want this war to be over everywhere. I want the men to come home and families to be back together." Louise sighed.

"That's what we all want, sweetheart. Even the families on the other side, I bet. I've got to think that there are German and Japanese families that don't want this war any more than we do and don't know all that is happening. Our enemies are fierce, Louise," Charles said, looking off in the distance out the window. "What they want, what they are, and what they do; it's all foreign to us. We don't understand them, and they don't like us. So, we fight. To keep things right. That's what we do," Charles said.

"I know, I know. It doesn't mean I have to like it. No more war talk. This is our anniversary! One year. Where do you think we'll be next year? In ten years!" Louise looked over at her husband and smiled.

"Ah. We'll be together with all those kids surrounding us," Charles said, finishing up his coffee and standing. "We're falling behind in that category, you know. All these people are having babies. We'll have one of our own soon," he said, pulling Louise to her feet.

"I'll be glad when we can do that. Let's pray this war is over soon. If I've got to have a household full, I'll need to get started," she said, laughing.

"It will be; I know it will be. The Japs can't hold out much longer. They have too much at risk, and we're right there on top of them," Charles said. "Okay, we'll cook dinner; what do you say? Then a movie?"

"Sounds great. Let's cook and surprise Mrs. Compton when she gets back from church. Then we go to the afternoon show. Hmmm. Now that you mention it, I want to see how Cary Grant wins the heart of Priscilla Lane," she said, batting her lashes. "Let's see if he's as good at it as you were."

"Uh-huh. One smile from you and I was done for; you know that. Wrapped around that little finger forever and ever. My main job in this marriage is to make you smile."

Louise pulled him close. "You are succeeding, my love. Happy Anniversary."

Tricia Cundiff

25

June 13, 1945

Dear Dad,

How are you making it in this hot weather? It sure is getting hot out here. Every morning it is cool and during the day you nearly burn up. The wind blows about 40 miles per hour all the time and this dust flies all the time.

Dad, I didn't forget that this Sunday is Father's Day. I tried to find you something I thought you might need but I couldn't' find you a thing so I will just send this bit of money so you can buy you a shirt or something. I am also going to have my subscription to 'Life' magazine sent home so you can have that, too.

I have been flying today; I sure like this B29. I had a letter from Sgt. Dalcomb Poag. He sure is a big shot now. I am sure proud of him and Joe both. I hope he gets home again before he has to go over.

Happy Father's Day-

Love, Charles

Tricia Cundiff

World War II

The spring of 1945 was a time of peril for the American forces fighting for control of Okinawa. The ground forces faced an enemy committed to Hirohito and the Japanese empire. Kamikaze pilots were the proposal the Japanese air commanders outlined in a desperate attempt to regain control of the war. The first attack of kamikaze pilots was in October of 1944; the numbers increased dramatically in 1945 during the Allied forces' pressure against Okinawa and the surrounding area. The suicide pilots crashed into ships and caused the greatest loss of the US Navy in a single battle, killing almost five thousand men. The kamikaze strategy allowed the use of untrained pilots and obsolete planes and aided in the short supply of gasoline because there were no return trips.

As word of the madness reached the families of the soldiers fighting in the Pacific, fears were heightened, and pressure was placed upon President Truman and Congress to end the war.

Amarillo, Texas

"Hondo? We're going to Hondo?" Louise looked at him, puzzled. "San Antonio?"

"No, we're not going. I'm going. Please stay here until I know where I'll be next. I'll talk to you every day if I can." Charles pulled her close to him. "Listen, it's only for a few weeks, then I'll be back here, or we'll go somewhere else. I don't know, Louise, I don't know for sure. You know the Army, I don't know anything until the last minute, it seems."

"Like Dalcomb," Louise said, leaning close to Charles, resting her head on his shoulder.

"Dalk will be okay. He is flying over there, you know. That's better than a ship; too many crazies fly bombs right into them. I don't know if he will get to go home before he goes over or not. I know Mother wants to see him. Well, Dad and Joe and Sarah, everybody wants to see him. I want to see him. But I guess I won't get a chance."

Louise could hear the sadness in his voice; she hugged him tighter. "He'll be okay. You both will. It's almost over; it has to be."

Charles pushed away the thought of never seeing Dalcomb again. He couldn't think like that; he had to believe what he had told his mother. He had to trust God. Dalk would come back, whole and complete. Truman had to do something. The war had to be over soon; rumors about the bomb were flying around the base. The crazy Japs and their kamikaze freaks. How do you fight crazy people that would sacrifice themselves for the likes of Hirohito?

Charles held onto Louise. He wanted to get away from all this talk when he could be with her, to leave it behind at the base and forget about it for a short while. But it followed them everywhere.

Sitting in the barracks with the other men, listening to the news they had heard from home, the gossip that flowed from one set of barracks to another, was exhausting. The reports of how terrible the Japanese prisons were and the horrific treatment of prisoners preyed upon the thoughts of every man on the base.

Charles looked down at the love of his life. He didn't want her to know what he heard, but he knew that news reports and rumors traveled quickly through the wives of the men on base. She probably heard the same things he did but didn't want to talk about them. When they were together, it seemed as if both wanted to leave that part outside their life for the short time they had.

"It's not quite dark yet, and it's cooled off a little. How about a little walk before dinner? We have tonight and most of the day tomorrow. I'm not going to leave next week; I'll be back next weekend. But it could be the next week. Come on, Hot Rock, no more frowns. Smiles are all I want to see," Charles said, pulling back and looking into the teary eyes of his wife.

"Yes," Louise said, smiling through the tears escaping down her face. She raised a hand to wipe them away. "You're here with me now; let's enjoy it."

Hondo, Texas

July 28, 1945

Dear Mother, Dad & all,

I have finished another hard week. I have studied more in the past two weeks than I ever have in my whole life. They are giving us so much stuff to learn in such a short time. There really is a lot of stuff you have to learn about a B29. We are learning how to figure out how much gas to carry to fly a long distance with a heavy load. The course is called Cruise control; you have to be able to tell how long, how much gas and how much bombs you can carry in a certain time to a given distance. It takes about three to four hours to figure out one problem and boy, that sure is hard to do for a whole week or two.

I guess I will finish up here in three more weeks. I have one more week of ground school and then two weeks of flying. I sure hope I get to come to Maxwell Field when I leave here, but I guess that would be too good.

I wrote Dalcomb a long letter today. I sure wish he would write me; I haven't heard from him in two or three weeks.

I also called Louise today; she is getting along fine and said to tell Sarah she said thanks a lot for the comforter. We really appreciate that.

Tell Joe I hope he can get into what he wants. Dad, this war news really sounds good.

Love, Charles

Sadie Compton, the landlady, sounded disappointed when she answered the phone. Charles supposed she wished that it had been her son. Charles told her that her son was in his prayers, and he was certain he could be there soon. Louise sounded breathless when she came to the phone.

"Chaz? Oh, honey, I'm so glad you called. I've talked to Sarah, and she said they missed a call from you. I think only Joe was home when you called. At least you got to talk to him!" Louise stopped to catch her breath.

"Whoa! What's wrong, sweetheart? Why are you so out of breath?" Charles asked.

"I had just left the house to walk down to the little market on the corner. Mrs. Compton, or Sadie as she insists I call her, caught me before I was too far away. She heard the market had some bananas; I wanted to get some before they were all gone."

"I suppose I could try and call you back if you need to go?" Charles said, joking.

"You better not hang up! Oh, Chaz, I hate this. At least when you were close by, I could see you every weekend. I'm going to try and come down next weekend, okay? I have some gas coupons," Louise replied.

"Let's wait and talk about it. I start flying soon for a couple of weeks, and then I think I will be finished here. Maybe I'll know more about where I'll go next, and we can figure it out," Charles said.

"You start flying? Already? I thought you were going to be in ground school for several more weeks," Louise said, her voice breaking.

"Oh yeah. They've been working us hard. I don't think the flying will be as bad as the ground school. I got a letter from Dalcomb, and I will send it home to Mother. He sounds okay; I guess he likes it as well as he can, considering where he is. He's either on the base or in the air, and he's safer there than he would be on a ship. The base over there isn't anything like we have here. Pretty rough, I think. But he sounds okay. I said

Love, Charles

that already, didn't I?" Charles said, leaning up against the wall where the phone hung. Hearing her voice was calming to his soul, he thought, smiling. He just wanted to hear her talk.

"Dalcomb will be okay, Chaz. He will; I just know he will. I really do want to see you, though. I work every day, but I miss you so much. Mrs. Compton is teaching me more things to cook. I want to cook you a really good dinner," Louise said, her voice catching.

"Sweetheart? What is it?" Charles said, concerned.

"Oh, I'm silly. I just miss you. All I want is for you to hold me. The same thing so many wives want right now. All this war news. We all want it to be over. Oh, you know about Joe, right?" Louise said, her voice sounding better, more relaxed.

"Good baby brother Joe. Yes, he's going to be a Navy man. I hope he gets into the aviation end of it. That would be the best thing right now. The Japs haven't got much of a fleet anymore; I don't think. We're getting pretty good at shooting them down," Charles said, wishing there were other things he could think of to talk about. Fear and indecision about the future clouded every conversation.

"Please, Chaz. It's not that far. Let's plan on me coming down there in the next couple of weeks, okay? I'll take off on Friday, be there on Saturday, and drive back home on Sunday," Louise said wistfully.

Charles knew how she felt. He wanted to see her, too, and they both could feel time slipping away, the future uncertain.

"Okay, we'll talk about it the next time I call. I'll have a better idea of what is going on, and I need to make sure that I can be off on Saturday. I love you, my Louise; I love you so much. But I've got to go; there's a line of guys here waiting on the phone," Charles said, nodding to the next guy in line.

"I love you, too, Chaz. So much. Call me soon. I'm writing you every day but only mailing them every other day. That's silly, I know. Okay, I know you have to go. I'll talk to you soon, my Chaz. Soon, okay?" Louise asked.

"For certain. Bye, sweetheart."

World War II

Japan refused to submit to the terms of the Allies Potsdam outlined for Germany's surrender. Three hundred thousand Japanese civilians were estimated to have died due to starvation or bombing raids by July 1945, but Japan's government showed no signs of surrender. Intelligence reports showed that Japan had deployed more than 560,000 soldiers and thousands of suicide planes to meet the invasion. The Japanese military intended to execute all American prisoners in Japan in the event of an Allied landing. American casualties weighed heavily on the mind of President Truman and Congressional leadership, as well as the Generals fighting on the front lines. Another dilemma facing Truman was timing. Only two atomic bombs were available for deployment; additional bombs would not be ready for weeks. A quick end to the war was needed; thousands of Chinese, American, and Japanese soldiers died each day the war raged on. President Truman approved the plan that allowed the Enola Gay, the plane piloted by Colonel Paul Tibbets, to drop the nuclear bomb nicknamed "Little Boy" on Hiroshima as the ultimate result of the bombing of pearl Harbor that had occurred on December 7, 1941. "Little Boy" landed on Hiroshima on August 4, 1945, and Truman, hearing of the bomb's successful detonation, shared the news with his advisors. The information was broadcast worldwide, and Allied servicemen breathed a sigh of relief; a death warrant on their lives had been lifted. American intelligence officers believed that two bombings in quick succession would convince the Japanese that Truman had multiple bombs at his disposal and would use them until Japan surrendered. The possibility of upcoming bad weather moved the date to drop the second bomb up to August 9, 1945.

'Bock's Car,' a B29 piloted by Major Charles W. Sweeney, loaded 'Fat Man,' the second bomb, and flew to Kokura, the primary target of 'Fat Man.' Clouds, along with Japanese antiaircraft, made Kokura an impossible drop zone. The pilot headed to the secondary target, Nagasaki. An opening in the clouds allowed for the dropping of 'Fat Man' and the detonation over Nagasaki.

Japan surrendered to the Allies on August 15 and signed the instrument of surrender on September 2, which ended the war. Debate continues on the ethical and legal justification for the bombings. Still, American families across the United States were looking for an end to the madness and anxious for their men to return home. Supporters of the military decisions made by President Truman and his generals, as well as the consent given by the United Kingdom to the bombings, believe they were necessary to bring an end to the war with minimal casualties. American military installations across the globe were anxious to deliver retaliation for the attack on Pearl Harbor. The American public could think of nothing further than their men coming home.

26

Texas

August 10, 1945

Dear Mother, Dad & all –

Sure has been a lot of things happening in the news in the last few days. I guess you have been listening to the news about Japan wanting to give up. I sure am glad things are going so good. I believe it will be over in a few weeks now, maybe Joe will never have to fight. I don't think I will get a chance either; that won't make me mad. I sure wish Dalcomb was over here instead of over there. However, I don't think he will have to do any fighting now. I hope not anyway.

I have been doing quite a bit of flying lately; we fly about five hours every day. I sure will be glad when I finish up here. I guess I will be leaving about August 20. I will let you know where I go. I guess I will be sent out to New Mexico or stay in Texas.

Tell Joe I am glad he got in the Navy. That is lots better than the infantry. I sure hope he can get on a carrier; I think he would like that better than anything else.

Love, Charles

"I couldn't let myself believe it until I heard it from you," Louise said. Charles could almost hear her smile and the twinkle in her eyes over the phone. Gosh, it had been too long since he had seen her. He felt guilty even thinking about their few weeks apart when so many had been apart for much longer.

"It's true. It's over. The Japs gave it up. There's still a lot to do over there, I guess. Dalk will probably have to stay over there for a while, and I might even have to go over, too. But there won't be fighting, anyway. Have you been listening to the radio?" Charles asked, holding the phone tight against his ear. The line behind him was getting longer; many men wanted to call and celebrate with their families, even if it was only through the phone.

"Yes, the radio is full of good news. They seem to be celebrating everywhere. It's really over. So now I just want to be with you. I'm coming this weekend; don't try to talk me out of it. I don't care if I only get to see you for a few minutes or hours," Louise said, her voice adamant.

"Sweetheart, I want you to come, but it's not a good time yet. Let me find out where I'm going, if I'm staying here. I don't want you to make this trip, and I don't even know where you would stay!" Charles was as anxious to see her as she was to come. He hated to tell her no; he wished he could leave and go to her.

"I don't have to worry about where to stay. Sadie has a friend there in San Antonio. I can sleep on her couch; I'll be fine," Louise argued.

"Louise, I'm sorry. I can't get out this weekend. Soon, I promise, soon. And we'll stay somewhere together. I don't want you on a stranger's couch," Charles replied.

"It's not a real stranger. I've talked to her on the phone. Sadie says she is a wonderful older lady and a great cook. She offered, Chaz!"

Love, Charles

"Okay, okay. It's a plan if we don't have another before you come. Just a couple of more weeks, Louise, okay?" Charles asked.

"I miss you so much," Louise answered, "but okay. Whatever you say. I'll keep working here until I can come. I'm saving some money; we'll have a little bit. Maybe we can stay one night somewhere together."

August 14, 1945

Dear Mother, Dad & all –

I guess August 14, 1945 will be remembered for a long time. I sure am glad this old war is over. Thank God this war is over. I guess Dalk will be coming home before long now. I sure am glad he didn't have to do much fighting.

I don't guess Dalk and I will be getting home too soon, I guess I will make up part of the Army of occupation since I haven't been overseas but that won't be as bad as fighting.

I heard the president while I was up flying in a B24 today. Maybe we can all be together by another year now. Tell old Joe he will probably have to go into the Navy but he sure won't have to do any fighting and the training will really be good for him.

Dalcomb will probably be home before me. I believe he will be home in a few months. I sure wish I could come home tonight. It is just hard to realize that this old war is over. Thank God, Thank God.

We will have to learn how to live all over again in peace times. You can buy all the meat and sugar you want. Tell Dad I guess that atomic bomb did the trick.

I will let you know where I am sent. Just had to write and tell you how glad the war was over.

Your son,

Charles

August 26, 1945

Dear Mother, Dad and all –

I expected to be away from here by now, but they decided since the war is over now they don't need us very bad so they are giving us two more weeks of school. I guess I will be ready to leave here around September 5 but I still don't have any idea where I will be sent.

I have had a couple of letters from Dalcomb, but he said he had never received any of our letters. I guess he really misses that mail. I know how you like to receive letters over here, and I am sure you would want mail twice as bad over there. He said he hadn't flown any missions so I guess he will get by without having to fly any now since the Japs surrendered.

Has Joe been called up by the Navy yet?

Louise is still getting along alright in Amarillo, she is still working. I sure do miss her, I will be glad when I leave here so she can follow me.

Love, Charles

Love, Charles

(from Louise to Charles' family):
August 29, 1945

Dear folks,

Here I am, still sitting up here in Amarillo. It looks like I'll be here until dooms day. Charley has been gone for seven weeks now, and it seems about like seven years.

I know you all were happy when the war was over. I can't realize that it is really over yet. There wasn't much of a celebration here. This town is a one-street town, and everyone gathered all along that street, with lots of horn blowing and yelling. That particular night they had the worst electrical storm that I have seen here and the rain came down in buckets. I had a two-day holiday which I enjoyed, but there was nothing for me to do but twiddle my thumbs.

I suppose Dalcomb will be home before long. Judy's husband hasn't said anything about coming home yet, but she looks for him at any time. Where is Mike now? I suppose Charley will have to go over eventually, but there is one consolation that they won't be shooting at him.

The lady I stay with and I are painting her kitchen. We just paint a little every night after we get home from work and it certainly is a tiresome job. This is my first time to ever paint anything, and hers too, so you can just imagine what it is going to look like when we get through. It at least helps to keep my mind occupied and I don't get quite so lonesome.

Has Joe had to go in the Navy yet? I had a letter from my brother Jack yesterday and he is still in the Pacific. His letter was written one day after peace was declared, and he said their celebration was very quiet.

I certainly hope Charley gets a furlough soon. We were at home just about this time last year, and I think it is time Charley was getting to go home again. He doesn't say much about a discharge, so I don't suppose he expects to get out very soon. I don't think it is anything but fair though to let these fellows out first that have been overseas for two and three years. Charley has been very fortunate and I thank God that he has been able to stay in the states this long.

I'll be so glad though when he is out or settled some place and we can start living like human beings. So many of the girls that work where I do, their husbands are getting discharges and they are all going home and getting ready to start raising a family. I really do envy them.

Take care of yourselves.

Love, Louise

Love, Charles

September 2, 1945

"My last day at work is Wednesday. I will start down Thursday and stop by to see Sadie's friend in San Antonio. I know you can't get free until Saturday, but I wanted to let you know in case you called me," Louise said. "I can stay with Sadie's friend until I get a place or until we know where we'll be going."

Charles smiled into the phone. He could hardly wait to see her. It had been so long. He wanted to plan something special but didn't know what to do. "That's good, sweetheart, be careful. I probably won't send you a letter this week, then. You wouldn't get it anyway. I just finished a letter to Mother. I told you about my Uncle Clarence, right? That's Aunt Freddie's husband. She's written me lots of times; I'll need to write her back, but I sure don't know what to say."

"Oh, I'm sorry, Chaz. I know you wish you could have been there. I met them; you know when we were home. What about Dalcomb? Have you heard from him?" Louise asked.

"Several letters have come from him, but he hasn't gotten any of mine. I'm not sure what's wrong with the mail over there. He still doesn't know when he will get to come back over. I think he will probably be able to get home before I will since he's been over there." Charles closed his eyes; he could hear Louise on the other end, just the slightest breath. It was enough; it had to be for now. But not for much longer. "I'm supposed to finish up here tomorrow, and then I don't know what I'll be doing. Since the war is over, they can't decide what to do with us. Did you listen to the radio last night?" Charles asked.

"Oh yes. Sadie and I sat right there to listen to that. I would imagine most of America was listening to the signing of the surrender. Oh, maybe I forgot to tell you. Sadie's son is back in the States. She's not sure when he'll get home; he's in a hospital close to DC. She's talked to him, at least. He barely escaped being killed. The Japanese were horrid to the prisoners, and the man that came by here said that the Japanese did horrible things that were against the Geneva convention and would have to pay for it. I don't know what he meant by that; how do they pay for something like that?" The catch in her voice made it clear that Louise was upset.

Charles chose his words carefully. He wanted to be there with her; dealing with evil was always much more difficult when you were alone. "I don't know, sweetheart. Let's be grateful that her son is coming home. He might need a lot of tending to. So, you won't get to meet him, will you?"

"No, not now, anyway. I told Sadie that we would try to get back up here to see her and her son; she's been truly good to me, Chaz," Louise said.

"Yes, she has. An angel to keep my sweet wife safe and cared for. I'll always be thankful for her," Charles replied, nodding to the Sergeant in the room. "I've got to get off the phone now, Louise. I'll see you Saturday morning at the main gate. It will be so good to see you. Are you all packed?"

"Almost. I love you, Chaz. A few days. It seems like it's been so long. Just a few more days. See you Saturday," Louise said.

"I'll be the tall one next to the gate with a big smile," Charles said. "I love you, too, baby,"

Handing the phone to the Sergeant, he asked, "Do you know anyone in Corpus Christi?"

Saturday morning, September 8

Charles was holding Louise in his arms for the first time in weeks; he wanted nothing more than to stand there breathing in her scent. She wiggled out of his arms, laughing.

"Oh, Chaz, it seems like such a long time. And now, now we don't have to be afraid anymore. This awful war is over. We don't have to be afraid of anything, do we? I was tired of always being afraid," Louise said, shaking her head and smiling into the face of the man she would travel around the world to be with.

"No, sweetheart, you don't need to be afraid any longer. The bad guys lost," Charles answered, pulling her back in his arms.

"Oh, the pictures were horrible. I don't even want to think about it. Why couldn't they have surrendered before then? The Japanese knew about the bombs. That's what they say on the radio. They knew, and they still didn't surrender. All those people, I just can't," Louise stopped, closing her eyes.

"No, don't think about that. The war is over. I'm sure there was bad, evil stuff from all sides in this horrible war. War is necessary sometimes, but there is always evil in it." Charles shook his head. "That's far away, and it's over. We'll be hearing a lot about it, I'm sure. But for now, it's you and me. And I have a surprise for you." Charles put his hand under his chin and tipped her face up to his. "I don't have to be back until late tomorrow afternoon. We're taking a little trip. Just down the road a bit. I know you drove all day yesterday, and I'll do the driving today."

Charles stared into the eyes he wanted to fall into forever. "Tonight, we have a room in Corpus Christi. We're off to the beach, Hot Rock. We have a room reserved at a little motel right on the beach. It took some doing, but I have a buddy who helped me. There's a naval base down there; they opened it in '39, I think. So, my buddy knew a guy there and reserved a motel room. It's just you and me, Louise." Charles looked at her, a question in his eyes.

"Nothing could be better than that," she replied, laughing.

Corpus Christi

The drive to Padre Island from Corpus Christi proved well worth it. Although there was little on the island, the beach and ocean views were beautiful and peaceful. Charles and Louise sat on a blanket a few feet from the water's edge and watched the waves lapping at the sand. Only a few others were on the beach; a couple with small children played in the water several yards away.

"I'm glad we drove over here," Louise said, leaning against Charles, her head nestled under his chin. "I wish we could stay for the sunset; I bet it's stunning."

"We'll be back one day. I promise we'll spend lots of time watching the waves and sunsets," Charles replied, enjoying the feel of his wife against him. Watching a small boat on the horizon, he realized he felt more peaceful at that very moment than he had in a very long time. Gone were the thoughts that invaded his dreams of bombs exploding in the air, of flying into battles.

Louise sat up and dug her toes into the sand. "We've got to leave soon, don't we?"

"Yeah, we do, sweetheart. I've got to get back. I'm sorry I kept you busy yesterday; we could have driven over here then and spent more time on the island," Charles said, grinning at his wife.

"That's quite all right, Mr. Poag. I believe I enjoyed myself just fine in that wonderful little motel room. Seeing the beach as soon as we walked out the door was wonderful!"

Charles laughed, and he stood and pulled Louise to her feet. "If we had ever walked out the door, I suppose we could have. Come on, let's take another walk. We'll go down that way this time," he said, pointing towards the pier. "Then we'll have time to stop and get something to eat before you drop me off."

"At least I'm going to be close by. I can see you again next weekend, right? I am going to try and find somewhere else to stay besides on this dear lady's couch," Louise said, shaking the sand from the blanket.

"Hold off on that a little. I'm hoping to hear something in the next day or two. I think we'll be able to go home for a few days, at least. No reason to rent something that you might only be in a few days, right?" Charles said.

"Oh, I hope it works out. So you'll call me as soon as you hear, right?" Louise asked.

"You know I'll call you as soon as I can," Charles said as he took her hand in his, as they walked down to the water, wading in the breaking waves.

"And call me if you hear from Dalcomb. I hope he'll be home soon. Your mother is worried; she wants him to be here, not out in the ocean somewhere." Louise reached down and picked up a shell. "A souvenir," she said, shaking the sand off.

World War II

American soldiers returning home from overseas after the end of the war were treated as heroes and welcomed with parades in communities and cities across the United States. There was a problem getting everyone home, however. With over seven million soldiers overseas, the promise to have the servicemen return home by Christmas was impossible. 'Operation Magic Carpet' began on September 6, 1945, and averaged transporting 22, 222 men home every day for almost an entire year. Aircraft carriers and other ships and planes were used as transport, the vessels and planes returning home at full capacity. Providing troops to remain on established posts in Germany and Japan was a problem faced by the military; servicemen protested redeployment in the Pacific and the military qualifications required for enlisted men to return home.

Tricia Cundiff

27

Texas

September 28, 1945

Dear Mother, Dad & Joe,

Well, here we are back in Texas again. We got in San Antonio Tuesday night and had quite a bit of trouble finding a place to stay that night. Then we came on out to Hondo Wednesday morning and got us a nice place to live out on a ranch seven miles from the field. We have a nice big room and Louise has kitchen privileges. It sure is nice out in the country. We have several horses and I go horseback riding every day. Also, there is plenty of squirrels around here so we can go hunting any time.

Mother, we didn't have a bit of trouble going down to Sarah's; we got there early Saturday morning. We drove all night Friday night. Uncle Cecil and Punk Taylor came over to Aunt Freddie's to see us. We left Sheffield about 10:00 o'clock Friday night and got at Sarah's about 9:00 o'clock Saturday morning. That Michael sure is a fine boy; he is the cutest kid I ever saw. I gave him sixty cents and he put the money in his pig. I think he liked me. They sure have a nice place to live and their apartment is really nice.

I had to buy another tire coming here from New Orleans. I have two new ones now.

I haven't found out what I am going to do here yet. We are just sitting around taking life easy. I guess I will find out something next week. I sure did enjoy being home. I believe I will probably be home to stay in about six months. I sure hope so anyway.

Love, Charles

"It just doesn't feel right, Chaz; I'm just not sure I can do this," Louise stared out the window from their room.

"But sweetie, it just doesn't make sense for you to try and find a job right now. We don't know what I'm going to do, where I'll be. There's nothing around here close. You would have to drive into San Antonio to find a decent job. No, please, forget about working for a bit. There is plenty to do right here. You love to ride! Buttermilk seems to have taken a liking to you. That horse doesn't want anything to do with me, but you come up, and he's all calm," Charles replied, walking up behind her and wrapping his arms around her waist.

"He's just a big baby; he likes the attention I give him," Louise said. She could see the horses just outside the stable from the window. They were grazing in the small field next to the house. Louise looked up at Charles. "I can't ride all day, every day."

"Of course not, but you know, you've got other things to do here. And until they find something for me to do, I'm here most of the time. I love the dinners you're cooking. I can't brag on you to my mother every single letter; she might get jealous if she knew you were cooking me things just as good as she does," Charles said, turning Louise around to face him.

Louise stood on tiptoe and kissed him on the lips softly. "It is nice to have you around, Mr. Poag." She nodded. "It might bother your mom a bit, but I imagine she's cooked so much lately that she's pretty tired of being in the kitchen."

"You're probably right about that. So many deaths, just so close to each other. First, Uncle Clarence, then Aunt Lilly. I

Love, Charles

think Mother has talked to Aunt Freddie several times since Uncle Clarence died. She said that Aunt Freddie is having a hard time, what with the kids and all. At least Aunt Lilly's kids are grown; Uncle Jess would have had a rough time with kids at home." Charles shook his head.

"I need a map to keep up with your family," Louise said. "I thought my family was big; maybe it's because it's easier to keep up with mine; yours seem to be spread out more."

"Maybe, but we have big families, don't we? People scattered around, but if we can get everybody home at one time, won't that be something? From your family and my family? We could have our own town, I think," Charles grinned.

"And just what would you call this town?" Louise asked, laughing.

"Well, Poagsville, of course," Charles said, joining Louise in laughter.

"My family would probably have something to say about that!" Louise replied.

"Okay, so maybe we call it Hot Rock Haven. That's it. Hot Rock Haven. You would be the mayor, of course, and I would fly around all day in my little cub and take people back and forth to the big city," Charles said, getting into the fantasy.

"There are many people I have a hard time imagining in your plane with you," Louise raised her eyebrows.

"Oh, they would get used to it. I could turn them upside down, flip them over, dip the wings a lot; yeah, they would all learn to love it." Charles spun Louise around.

"What about Dalcomb? Doesn't he like to fly, too?" Louise asked.

"He would be my co-pilot. And we would live on a big lake, and Joe would take people across the lake to the other side on some big fancy ship he would have, you know, being in the Navy and all," Charles answered.

Louise laughed, sitting down and taking a deep breath. "How is he? Joe? Didn't you say he was having a tough time of it?"

Charles nodded, the fantasy slipping away. "Yeah, that's what I hear. I think book camp is kicking his butt. But it will be good for him. He's been riding big in high school. Time for him to come back down to earth. And he's not going into war; that's the best thing. I hoped I would hear from him before I wrote Mother, but I probably won't."

"I need to write a couple of letters myself. Did you ask your mother to send that cucumber recipe? Mrs. Jenkins wants a copy of it, too. I'm going to try it; we got a lot of pickling cukes ready." Louise asked.

"Yes, I told her to send it. I hope she goes to the doctor soon. She's been having trouble with her leg for too long, and she said she was going to wait for cooler weather to get it fixed," Charles replied.

"Sure, I'll believe it when she does it. Your mother doesn't take very good care of herself; she's too busy taking care of everyone else! But don't worry," she said, seeing the look on Charles' face, "your dad will make her go if it gets too bad."

"All right, enough of this. Back to Hot Rock Heaven. Madame Mayor, would you like me to saddle up Buttermilk for you? The sunset will be beautiful." Charles held out his hand for his wife.

"Madame Mayor's husband? Yes, I think I would like that very much. But first," she said, pulling his face to hers, "I need some personal royal attention."

October 28, 1945

Dear Mother & Dad,

How is everything around Armour these days. I have been receiving quite a bit of mail this past week, I had a letter from Dalcomb and he is just fine. He said the storm was pretty bad and that it blew away his mess hall so they have been having trouble getting food to eat. But he was making it just fine. He and another boy have built them a pretty nice house. I guess you have heard from him by now. I will send his letter to you.

I had a letter from Joe and one from Sarah also. I guess old Joe is catching it pretty hard in boot camp. Those first ten weeks sure are hard. I never will forget Keesler Field, Mississippi. That training will really do old Joe some good. He will know just how tough the Navy is and also how many bosses you can have over you. Sarah said they were getting along just fine.

I still don't have any idea when I will leave here or where I will go; I am not doing much, just going to school about four hours a day. We went to church this morning; we go nearly every Sunday morning.

Love, Charles

"Look at my beautiful wife! This is a surprise," Charles said, sliding into the driver's seat as Louise moved over to the passenger side. "What's that in the back?"

"Just a little basket with a couple of sandwiches. For a picnic. Let's go over to the rise behind the airfield. I've seen other people over there playing with their children. I think we can have a picnic there," Louise said. Charles took the car most days when he needed to report early to base, but today she had asked that he let her drive and pick him up so she could run some errands.

"So, this is the surprise, huh? This is your errand? To fix us a picnic? That is so good of you, sweetheart," Charles said, a little confused. The view from the ranch where they lived would be much better, but he didn't want to complain.

Charles pulled out an old blanket from the trunk and spread it across the only grassy area. The noise from the airfield was louder than expected, and he could see the disappointed look on Louise's face.

"It's okay, Louise. It will probably get better in a few minutes. They did have some exercises scheduled this afternoon," he said, hoping to reassure her.

"Oh, my, this is not turning out as I wanted," Louise said, sitting down on the blanket and immediately swatting at flies that were determined to land on the sandwiches. She saw Charles swat at a mosquito, and a tear rolled down her face.

"Oh, sweetheart, what is it? Don't get upset! Come on; we can wrap up our sandwiches, go back to the ranch, and have a picnic there. Mrs. Jenkins won't mind. Look, you even have enough for her and her daughter?" Charles was even more confused at Louise's reaction.

"I wanted us to be alone. I didn't want to be where there was anyone else," Louise started, shaking her head.

"Oh, my sweet wife. Don't cry," he said, reaching over and wiping a tear from her face. "What's going on? Is there something wrong you need to tell me?"

Louise took a deep breath. "No, nothing's wrong. It's all wonderful. I just wanted it to be perfect when I told you." She reached over and put her hands on each side of his face. "I'm pregnant. We're going to have a baby!"

The shocked look on Charles' face frightened her. Then she saw his smile. Of course, it was a shock. But he was happy; she could tell he was happy.

Charles jumped up and immediately stepped on the pack of sandwiches. "Oh, look what I did. I'm so sorry; I didn't mean to," he said, leaning down and pulling Louise to her feet. "Thank you, uh, this is wonderful, you're right. Oh no," he said, looking down at the mess on the bottom of his foot and the ruined food on the blanket. The smile never left his face. He spoke again, but the sound of the plan above drowned out his words. He saw Louise shaking her head, pointing to the sky, and pulled her close to him. Holding her tight, he waited until the plane had passed over.

The sound receded into the distance, and he whispered in her ear. "I didn't think there was a way for you to make me happier. I was wrong. Seeing the joy on your face makes me so happy. And, of course, wow, what can I say? We made a baby!"

"Our baby, yes, Chaz, our baby. I'm so glad you're happy about it," Louise said, placing her head on his chest.

"Of course, I'm happy! Me and you, Hot Rock, and Baby Hot Rock!" Charles laughed and looked down at the ruined picnic. "I think I might have ruined your plans a little."

"It's okay; I don't think I could eat right now anyway," Louise said, snuggling into his arms. "We're going to have a baby. Our family, it's growing."

"Yep, Hot Rock Haven will have a new resident."

Tricia Cundiff

28

Hondo, Texas

November 12, 1945

Dear Mother & Dad,

I had a nice birthday, Louise cooked me a nice cake and Sarah sent me a box of candy. Also, the lady we live with baked a chicken with dressing, so I had plenty to eat.

Joe wrote me this week. He seems to be doing alright in the Navy now. I believe he will like it lots better after he gets through his boot training. I guess he will get home for a furlough by Christmas.

I haven't heard from Dalcomb but once since I have been here. I believe he will be home by the first of the year or in 3 or 4 months anyway.

We are still just fine. I am still not doing much, just going to school and laying around. I guess I will probably be moved from here before long. It looks like this field may close and if I leave here, I will go up to Denver, Colorado. If I possibly can I sure am going to try and get home for Christmas if I can possibly get a leave.

We haven't received the cake you sent yet but I am expecting it tomorrow. I sure will enjoy it, I haven't had a fruit cake since last Christmas.

Be good,

Charles

"You didn't say anything about the baby," Louise said, handing the letter back to Charles after reading it.

Charles smiled. "No, I didn't. I want to tell them on the phone, not in a letter. Have you talked to your mom yet?" He asked, guessing she had not told her family yet.

"No, you're right. I want to tell them over the phone. I want to hear the happy, you know?" Louise said, grinning back at him.

"Okay, so what about tonight? We've kept it to ourselves pretty well so far; maybe it's time we tell the world how happy we are so they can be happy for us," Charles asked.

"Let's wait until tomorrow. I'm going to the doctor on base tomorrow to see if I can get something for this morning sickness. I'm scared to eat much any time of day because I know what it's going to feel like when I get up," Louise complained.

"Oh, sweetheart. I'm so sorry you're sick. It's almost every day, isn't it?" Charles wrinkled his nose at her.

"Every day. Every single day. This little one is changing things in there, I guess." Louise patted her flat belly. "I think I'm a little bit bigger. My slacks feel a little tight," she said hopefully.

"Oh, Hot Rock. I don't see even a little bump. But it's sweet that you want that baby to push out your tummy," Charles laughed.

"Of course I do. I want everyone to look at me and say, "Look! They've started on their eight children, finally!"

Charles laughed harder. "Maybe we need to rethink that whole eight children thing," he said, pulling Louise to his lap.

"You think? Okay, maybe we'll cut down on the number a bit," she said as she hugged him.

"This doctor, he's on base, right? That's what you said," Charles said. "I'm glad you're going to the doctor, but you know, we'll probably be somewhere else soon, and you'll have to go to another one."

"Have you heard something?" Louise leaned back and looked at him.

"They're talking about closing the base by the end of the year. We'll have to go somewhere. They're not going to just let me out; I don't think. We've been here a while, you know."

Louise shrugged. "It's all okay. I go where you go. I'm happy no one is talking about sending you overseas. I want you here for this baby."

"I plan on being right here if there is any way they will let me," Charles replied.

November 25, 1945

Dear Mother & Dad,

I am still sitting here going to school. They are closing this field December 31, so I guess I will be shipped out before long. I don't have any idea where I will be sent. I guess it will be Denver, Colorado if they have room for us there. I sure have been here a lot longer than I thought I would. I guess they are trying to make up their minds what to do with us. I wish all your beliefs of me coming home was true. But you will have to tell the Army they don't need us, and that's a pretty hard job.

These are pictures Dalcomb sent to Sarah and she sent them on to me. Sarah said he didn't say where they were made. The one of the airplane is a B25 so I guess that is the plane he is on.

Louise has been sick for the last two weeks. She gets sick every morning (haha) so I guess you will have another grandchild before long. I sure want a little rough neck boy.

But I guess we will get a girl. Louise is taking some kind of shots and they help her a lot.

I have heard from Joe this week and he said they were pretty crowded in their new barracks. I guess he will have it lots easier after he finishes there. I believe this Navy training will really help him.

That fruit cake sure was good. That is the best fruit cake I ever saw for a bought cake.

Love, Charles

Charles was trying to concentrate on the chalkboard at the front of the class. It was hard to listen to the instructor; everyone in the class had heard the same lecture before. Maybe some of them didn't get it the first time, he thought. Of course, it didn't hurt to have refreshers on plane maintenance; the differences between one plane and another were vital in their upkeep.

The instructor paused as a sergeant walked in and pointed in Charles' direction. "Poag? Come with me, please," the Sergeant said.

As Charles rose, the Sergeant continued. "Bring your stuff; you won't be back in here today."

Confused, Charles rose, grabbed the small bag he had sitting next to the chair, and nodded to the man sitting next to him. "I'm not sure what this is about," he said to no one in particular. The other men in the class were watching him, concerned. It was usually bad news when you were called out of class.

Charles hurried down the hall, following the quick-stepping Sergeant in front of him. Stopping at the double doors that led outside the building, the Sergeant turned and placed his hand on Charles' shoulder. "Go on over to the clinic. Your wife is there, and I think maybe they will take her over to San Antonio. She's okay, man," the Sergeant said at the stricken look on

Charles' face. "But she wants you with her, and it's all been cleared."

Less than thirty minutes later, he and Louise were headed to San Antonio. Holding Louise's hand in the back of the ambulance, he tried to quiet the voice still ringing in his head; the doctor quietly telling him that he thought the baby was in trouble.

Louise moaned and gripped his hand tighter. "Oh, sweetheart, hang in there. I'm right here. We'll be there soon; maybe they can give you something that will help." Charles didn't know what to say, how to comfort her.

Louise looked up at him, tears streaming down her face. "It's okay; I'm okay. I'm just so worried about our baby. The poor little thing, oh please, God," she said as another pain sliced through her. As the agony passed, she continued. "It started this morning. I thought I might get through a day without becoming nauseous, but it suddenly hit me. Not like the other mornings, just a shooting pain in my side. I knew something was wrong. Mrs. Jenkins brought me directly to the doctor. Poor woman, I'm sure she thought I would die on the way; I made such a fuss. But oh, Charles," she said and gripped even harder on his hand as another pain sliced through her, "I'm so scared."

"We're going to pray, Louise, just like you said last night, you know? We're going to pray for our family, our baby," Charles said, holding her hand with both of his, rocking as the ambulance took a quick turn.

Louise nodded and closed her eyes. The mumblings of each as they prayed brought tears to the eyes of the attendant who sat on the other side of Louise, monitoring her breathing.

Tricia Cundiff

Monday, December 3, 1945

Dear Mother & Dad,

I guess Judy called you and told you about Louise being in the hospital. I meant to call you but Judy said she would call you so I figured that would be just as good because I was going to write you today.

Louise was pregnant as I told you, and she had been going to the doctor taking shots so she wouldn't be sick all the time. Then she got a pain in her side. So the doctor examined her and thought the baby was growing in the improper place so he sent us to another doctor and he thought the same thing. There is no way to x-ray so they had to operate to see what was wrong. When they got inside they found the baby was alright but that she had bad appendixes so they took them out. She is getting along just fine, they gave her the shot in the spine and she didn't have to take ether so she wasn't sick at all. She was operated on Saturday morning and Sunday night they let her eat a little. She was feeling real good today. They let her sit up and eat herself. The nurses here are surprised that she feels so well in such a short time. I think she will be up walking in a few days.

I hope we can get home for Christmas but I don't guess I will have much to say. The Army takes care of its men pretty well. I heard from Dalcomb, Sarah and Joe. They are all fine. Maybe Joe will be home by New Years. I hope Sarah and Mike will get to come.

I will let you know if anything goes wrong. I think Louise will be all right in a little while and the doctor thinks she will keep the baby alright.

Love, Charles

"Lieutenant Poag, Sir?" The young man gently shook Charles' shoulder. Charles had been sleeping, although fitfully, on the short couch in the waiting room. Louise was sleeping, and he didn't want to disturb her. Thankful he had been able to stay close by, he knew that she needed rest and took quick naps so that he could be there when she was awake.

Charles woke quickly, realizing the man was speaking to him. "Sir, they want you to come to your wife's room."

Charles jumped up quickly, running to Louise's room, leaving his shoes beside the couch. Pushing open the door, he didn't see Louise. Looking around, the only person in the room was a nurse, changing the sheets on the bed.

"Where is she? Where is Louise?" he asked, frantic.

The matronly woman with the nurse's uniform turned and walked to him. "Charles, sit down. She's okay, they've taken her downstairs, but she'll be back soon." The nurse, Emma Stanton, had been with them since they first came onto the hospital floor and tried to help as much as possible.

"But what's wrong?" Charles said, sitting in the chair that Emma Stanton had moved from the side of the bed.

"Now you just be calm, boy. That little one, the wee baby, couldn't make it. Your wife, she's had a miscarriage, and she's a might upset. I know your heart is breaking, too, but you must be strong for your wife now. There will be other babies, but this baby is gone with God now," the nurse said as she laid her hand on his shoulder. Looking down at him, tears rolled down her face. She had become close to these two since they had landed on her floor, and she hated to see such fine people face such tragedy in a world that had seen enough pain over the past few years.

Charles felt a heavy weight descend as if someone had handed him a stone that he couldn't bear to hold up. Louise was his life; the baby was their future. He didn't know how to deal with this. Death wasn't new to him, but this was something past grieving a death. Sobs broke through, and he fell to his knees. "Oh, God, our baby. Louise, my wife. Please, God, I don't know what to do. Help her; please make her be okay. Help me to help her. Oh, no," he sobbed, not knowing what to say.

"That's all good, now," Nurse Stanton said. "God knows your heart. He knows what you need, and He'll provide it. Your Louise, she's going to be fine. It was early on, so she could bounce right back from this in her body. You've got to help her heart and help her find God in this pain. Sometimes it's hard to find our faith when it's tested like this, so you help her with that."

Charles shook his head. He was having a hard time hearing God's voice. Instead, he heard his mother's. 'You wait on God to tell you what to do, son. Sometimes that's all we got.'

29

Hondo, Texas

December 17, 1945

Dear Mother & Dad,

I am suppose to be working in a office here at the base so being I don't know anything about office work I just sit around and do nothing. I thought I would just type you a letter for practice.

Louise is getting along just fine. I took her home yesterday, she is up walking around. I bought her a girdle and she wears that while she is up. The doctor said she would be able to travel by Wednesday so I guess I will be leaving here before long. I was suppose to leave last Thursday but they let me stay until she got able to travel. I was suppose to go to Houston, Texas, but I don't know where I will be sent now.

Mother, don't send any packages or anything here because I guess I will be leaving here before long. I am still going to try and get a leave when I leave here but I don't much expect to get one.

Mother, I don't want you to worry about Louise. I am sure those shots didn't have anything to do with her losing the baby. I had two good doctors and I know they know more than you and I. She had bad appendix and if I had waited until later she may have died instead of just losing the baby. I am sure we did the right thing. I think when you ask God to help you He will tell you the right thing to do.

I have heard from Dalcomb since he has been in Japan. He was doing just fine. I think he likes Japan better than he did Okinwa. I haven't heard from Joe; I guess he sure will be glad to get home. I sure would like to see him in those bell bottom trousers.

I am having to pay for the operating. It cost me $300 but I had a insurance policy on Louise that just about pays me that all back.

Daddy, take care of yourself and don't work too hard. I thought you would write me a letter after I sent you those GI shoes. How are they doing these cold days? I read in the paper that you was having a little snow in Tennessee these days.

Love, Charles

"Hi, sweetheart. How have you been today?" Charles asked as soon as he walked up to the porch. Louise was sitting in the rocker, a light blanket around her shoulders. "Are you cold? It's mighty warm out here," he said, concerned.

"No, I'm good. It's beautiful out here, isn't it? It was a little chilly when I came out; a breeze was coming off the plain." Louise looked across the field; the horses were grazing within sight of the house. "I wish I could go riding."

Charles sat down next to her. "I think that might be a while. Has today been okay? I tried to get home as soon as I could. It is so boring in that office. Nothing to do but sit all day. That's what most people on base seem to be doing now, just waiting."

"Yes, Chaz, I'm okay. Did you mail my letter? I wish everyone would stop worrying about me. All the letters are about how I feel and about the baby. I'm so tired of everyone saying it was for the best and will be different next time. I write back and say I'm fine, but I can't say anything else. No one would understand," Louise sighed.

"I do. I do, sweetheart. Our baby is gone. Our baby is in heaven. It doesn't matter that the little one was only just started; we didn't get a chance to hold our baby. Everybody wants to try and make you feel better Louise; that's all." Charles had grieved the loss also, but he knew he couldn't take the grief away from his wife. They both needed to grieve and heal.

"I know, I know. I feel so, so empty," Louise said, placing her hand on her stomach. "Even though I wasn't showing yet, I knew that little life was inside me."

Charles placed his hand over hers. "There will be life there again, someday. We will always remember the little life waiting for us in heaven, and we will still be thrilled with the new life God gives us."

"I can't think about that now," Louise said, shaking her head.

"Oh, I know; I'm sorry. I'm just like the rest of them, I guess. I want to say something to make you feel better," Charles apologized.

"No, no. You hurt, too. I know you do, and I'm not much good at trying to make you feel better." Louise took the blanket from around her shoulders and folded it. "Let's not talk about it anymore, not right now. Let's talk about something else, Chaz."

"Oh, my goodness. I forgot. See what you do to me, Hot Rock? I see you sitting up here, and I completely forget the most important thing I was bringing home." Charles pulled an envelope from his pocket. "I got my orders. I haven't opened it yet; I thought we should do this together. As a matter of fact, I think you should read it first."

"Silly," Louise said, reaching for the envelope, then holding it in her lap. Looking around at the high grass blowing gently in the wind and one of the horses nuzzling the other. "I will be a little sad to leave this place, Chaz. I'm leaving so much behind here," she said, a catch in her throat.

Charles didn't say anything. There was nothing to say. The hopes and dreams they had lain in bed and talked about, the names they had considered for their child would remain here and in their memory.

"Okay, let's see where we're going," Louise said, tearing open the envelope. "Lieutenant Charles Poag, report to Squadron H, Selman Army Air Force, Monroe, Louisiana." She looked over at her husband. "Where is Monroe, Louisiana?"

"Ah, it's up in the northern part. About halfway to home, I think. A lot closer, anyway. When does it say I report?" Charles asked.

Louise read further into the letter, a smile on her face. "You got a leave. We can leave on Saturday, Chaz. You're released on Saturday, the 22nd, at noon, and you don't report to Monroe until Tuesday, January 8. We can go home," she said, with tears in her eyes.

Charles smiled at the love of his life. He saw so much sadness in the eyes that he adored, sadness, with maybe just a touch of hope.

Louisiana

January 13, 1946

Dear Mother & Dad,

I guess you figure I am pretty bad about writing. When we got here about 2:30 Sunday afternoon we couldn't even find a place to stay overnight. We finally found a tourist court. Monday I just started out asking at every house for a place to live and I found a nice room with a private bath so I guess we are pretty lucky.

Louise is getting along just fine now. I believe she is getting back some of her strength.

It looks like I will get out of the Army in a few weeks now. I believe I will be out by the first of March any way.

I sure had a nice time while I was home and I sure was glad I got to see Joe. I guess he got back to camp alright. From the talk on the radio it looks like Dalcomb will get to come home before very long now.

Love, Charles

January 19, 1946

Dear Mother & Dad,

Received your letter today. We also got our sausage and boy it sure is good. We eat sausage for breakfast, dinner and supper. Thanks a lot but I didn't expect you to send it so soon after we left.

It is still raining here nearly everyday. In fact it has rained every day but 3 days since we have been here. I am not doing anything but just sitting here. They don't have our orders from Hondo yet so I don't have a single thing to do.

I sure was glad Joe got back alright. Let me know if he has changed his address. I want to write him.

I heard from Dalcomb and he is getting along just fine. Louise is also doing just fine. I believe she will be alright in a little while. We like our place to live. It is pretty nice.

Love, Charles & Louise

Charles stood at the window, his arms around Louise, watching the trees move. The patter of rain on the roof from above was calming, lending peace to the view outside. The hard splatter had slackened to a gentle shower, the sun peeking through the clouds above. Charles thought there was a rainbow somewhere, although it wasn't visible from their window. He supposed it was like their life. They would survive; they would feel the loss less, hopefully, each day and be able to find their own rainbow. He pulled Louise closer to him.

His wife was getting stronger each day, bringing her closer to her old self. The ache for their child in heaven would remain, but God's promises helped to ease the pain and look to the future.

"You're home early," Louise said. "I was thinking of maybe looking around for a job the first of the week. I feel like I'm ready. I need to do something."

"No need. We have a new adventure ahead of us. Our new journey doesn't start here." Charles said, resting his head on top of hers.

Love, Charles

Tricia Cundiff

30

Dear Mother & Dad,

We're coming home.

Love, Charles

Lt. Charles Hugh Poag served in World War II attached to the Strategic Air Command from 1943 to 1946. He was recalled during the Korean War as Pilot Engineer on B-36 bombers from 1951 to 1953. He was a member of the 492nd squadron of the SAC.

EPILOGUE

Charles died on February 1, 1995, of a massive heart attack. He was at home with Louise, his wife of over 50 years, at his side. Louise met her Chaz again on January 6, 2007, after suffering a brain aneurysm. Both had requested that their bodies be donated to Vanderbilt Medical School for research. Afterward, per their requests, their ashes were joined together as one for eternity.

Their wide gold wedding bands – the same ones made from cadaver gold – were melted together to form two wide bands for us, their daughters. Before the big meltdown, we decided to include bands that our husbands had given us. We now have the blended golden bands of love that join our hearts together. We are the recipients of a loving father and mother, and the joys and guidance they gave us make us thankful for each moment we have on this earthly plain, knowing that we will see them again. But that's not the end of the story.

When Tricia, who has journeyed through the letters as an observer from outside the family clan, requested that we write the epilogue to the story, we agreed to bring the story up to date from the ending of the letters. But, oh, what a story we have witnessed!

Seeing the letters brought to life through this book has been a two-year journey that has blessed both of us, and we hope, will bless many others. Our thankfulness for our grandmother's wisdom and love in keeping the letters she cherished, gave us an insight into our parents that we never would have had otherwise. Tricia's research of the World War II culture recalled the fear and loss many endured during these tumultuous times.

Charles and Louise wrote wartime letters to each other, and when the war was over, burned those letters. They later expressed their sorrow at doing so, and wished they had them to pass on to us. The letters Charles wrote to his mother, our grandmother, will always be a precious heirloom to be passed down through the generations of the Poag and Ramsay families.

Charles and Louise made their home in Knoxville, Tennessee, after living in Armour for a short time when they returned home. Charles graduated from the University of Tennessee with a degree in Civil Engineering. He reminded Joe often that the slide rule was what got him through college. Employed first by Mason Dixon and then with the Dupont Company, Charles moved with Louise to Kinston, North Carolina, and then to the Old Hickory, Tennessee facility of DuPont, where he and Louise made their home for many years.

Louise graduated with a degree in Psychology from Belmont College in 1969 at the age of 48, earning her Master's degree at Fisk University in 1971. Retiring from Metropolitan Nashville Schools in 1984 as a school psychologist, she continued her love for child psychology by consulting with local medical doctors.

Charles and Louise continued their love of learning by becoming lifelong students auditing classes at Vanderbilt Divinity School and University, Peabody and Aquinas Jr College, instilling a love of books and learning in us, their daughters. Both remained lifelong church members, serving as Sunday School teachers and council members. After retirement, Charles and Louise traveled extensively, moved to a condominium, and remained in the Nashville area, close to their daughters. Charles suffered from debilitating arthritis, and swimming alleviated some of that discomfort. He and Louise swam laps at the local YMCA, never swimming together but watching each other for safety. Charles called Louise his Ester Williams, and she named him her Johnny Weissmuller. Charles reminded her often that she was still his 'Hot Rock.' Each Christmas they were together brought stockings filled with apples, oranges and nuts for each other. Thankfully, Santa told them that their girls preferred bubblegum. But that's not the end of the story.

Our mother and father left us with precious memories, laughter, and a love for God, family, and country. We are thankful to Avery Green for that blind date he set up many years ago for our father. Charles often commented that he still owed Avery one hundred dollars on the bet he and Avery had made (recounted in the story). Avery was positive that Charles would find this young secretary appealing and would like her. Charles, with a twinkle in his eye, would look at his beloved Louise and say he hadn't decided yet whether he liked her or not.

Knowing that our father left this one thing undone, we finally located Avery Green's daughters, Flo Green Overstreet who lives in Old Hickory, Tennessee and Marion Green Earwood in Universal City, Texas. By this book's publication, Charles Poag's debt to Avery Green will have been paid, with our tears of gratitude for precious lives lived, loved, and blessed.

Jennie Poag Brown   *Priscilla Poag Wanamaker*

P. S. Thank you to Jackie Preston for being the first step in making these letters come to life and Tricia Cundiff for truly living them.

Charles Hugh Poag
11/7/1921 – 2/1/1995

Maxie Poag with her boys (left to right)
Joe, Charles and Dalcomb

Hugh White Poag, 10/9/1883 – 3/25/1966
Maxie Lee Bishop Poag, 3/5/1890 – 5/20/1981
Married 4/10/1919 (Photo taken in 1943)
Charles requested that his mother send him a picture of her and his father. This is the photo Charles received and kept by his cot in the barracks.

Charles' brother, Dalcomb Poag, died at the age of 82. Married to his sweetheart for fifty-five years, Dottie Catron of Gallatin, Tennessee. He attended the University of Tennessee after his service in World War II and retired from the United States Postal Service. He and his wife had no children.

Sarah Poag Cannon, the older sister of the Poag brothers, died at the age of 94. She and her husband, Mike, had been married for 63 years at the time of Mike's death. They had three boys, Michael, Bruce, and Scott Cannon. They made their home in Louisiana, and the boys run the family business that started many years ago.

Little Brother Joe Poag died at age 87. He was married to the love of his life, Peggy Weatherford of Murfreesboro, TN, for 62 years. After his service in the Navy in World War II, Joe graduated from the University of Tennessee with a degree in accounting and retired as owner of Ozburn-Hessey Company in 1985. He and Peggy had two sons, Mark and Jim. Mark is semi-retired from the company, and Jim has retired, enjoying farming and fishing. Family members remain working at the company.

Charles and Louise (1944)

Charles and Louise (early 1950s)

Charles with Louise's sister, Judy

Louise with Charles' brothers,
Dalcomb and Joe

Judy, on her way to see Charles & Louise in Amarillo, TX (left).

Judy's husband, Frost in front of barracks (below).

Judy, Louise's sister, and confidante, suddenly passed away at age 64. She and her husband, Frost, had three children, Donna, Jimmy, and Peggy.

Louise's oldest sister, Elizabeth, and her husband, Hubert – 1930s. Elizabeth married Hubert McCollum in 1931; they were married for 57 years at his death. Several years after Hubert's death, Elizabeth and her Old Hickory/DuPont High school sweetheart rekindled their love at age 80 and were married. Elizabeth died at the age of 82.

Louise's mother with her two oldest siblings – Elizabeth and Curry. This is the only known picture of Curry – the little boy with the curls on the right, made in the early 1900s. Curry Ramsay, the oldest brother of Louise, served in the military during World War II and married Roxie after the war. They had no children.

Jack Ramsay

Jack, Louise's baby brother and traveling companion until he had to get back to his sweetheart, Charlene, died at age 91. Jack served in WWII in the Navy aboard the USS Shields in the South Pacific. He and Charlene were married for 64 years and had two sons, Chuck and Carter Ramsay.

Jack and his sweetheart, Charlene with Louise's parents, Jim and Jennie Belle Ramsay (1940s)

Charles Hugh Poag, recalled during the Korean War

Charles & Louise, at home in Nashville, TN, 1993

Louise's picture in the church directory. She said that it was a tough one to have done, the first one taken after her Chaz's death.

Louise, a few months before her death in 2007. She had mentioned a wish to love on a horse again and hear it neigh. A thoughtful family friend, Patsy Templeton, and her horse, Lincoln, made that happen by coming to Louise's home.

'Jen & Tonic'
Charles and Louise continued horseback riding throughout their lives, and passed along their love of horses to their daughter, Jennie. This is Jennie with her horse, Tonic. Priscilla opted for horse-powered muscle cars.

Avery Green, 9/28/1920 – 7/24/2007
It is only fitting that Avery Green is recognized in this array of photographs, for without him, the tale would not have included the love story. We are thankful that Avery Green played Cupid.

Charles' and Louise's girls, Priscilla (left) and Jennie, 1958.

Jennie Poag Brown (left) born 1949, and Priscilla Poag Wanamaker born 1953. The Poag/Ramsay lineage ends here for Charles and Louise. Their daughters, Jennie and Priscilla, have no biological children yet experience the love of children's laughter often through their marriages and the children of relatives. The stories and family pictures remain for all the Poags and Ramsays to carry in their hearts.

Made in the USA
Coppell, TX
06 December 2022